ANARCHISM

Consulting Editors

The Editor

R O B E R T   H O F F M A N   is Assistant Professor of History at the State University of New
York at Albany. He received his A.B. at Harvard
and his M.A. and Ph.D. at Brandeis. Dr. Hoffman
has recently finished a book on Proudhon. He is
also the author of numerous articles on political
and social thought.

ANARCHISM

EDITED BY
Robert Hoffman

ATHERTON PRESS

New York 1970

Contents

ANARCHISM

Introduction

ROBERT HOFFMAN

Anarchy means the complete absence of government and law.

Government is instituted to create and preserve order in society and to protect people from violence done them by their neighbors or foreigners.

Therefore, anarchy must mean the complete absence of order and protection—chaos.

Anarchism is a theory which advocates anarchy.

Therefore, anarchism advocates disorder and violence—chaos.

This seems logical. The premises appear to make the conclusions inescapable.

But anarchists claim that just the opposite is true. *They* say that a society ruled by government can not be orderly, that government creates and perpetuates both disorder and violence.

Government is anarchy! wrote Proudhon, an anarchist who loved paradox.

Apparently there is an abyss in meaning between anarchists and conventional thinking about what they advocate. The political climate has rarely been conducive to a crossing of this gap, so that anarchism has been talked about far more than it has been understood.

Anarchists have been viewed at best as rather foolish idealists; more often they have been regarded as dangerous, even frightening threats to the maintenance of justice and social tranquility. There is a real basis for these fears, but historically the popular image of anarchists has most often been gross caricature.

People usually have associated them with revolutionary violence, which at one time was advocated by many anarchists. Terrorism and assassination were often thought to be virtually synonymous with anarchism, although actually anarchists rarely committed such acts. Attributed to them—sometimes falsely—were a number of notorious incidents of bomb-throwing and the killing of public officials, crimes that did much to form this popular image.

To this association of anarchism with violent incidents were added other, largely fantastic, notions created mainly out of anxiety, fear, and ignorance; anarchists were regarded as the most terrifying and hateful of people. These attitudes were often exploited and intensified by politicians, police officials, and newspapers seeking scapegoats for a variety of social ills and popular unrest.

For years it was common to condemn political opponents of many different sorts as "anarchists"—the ultimate term of opprobrium—and to blame most violence and civil disorder upon anarchists. After the Bolshevik Revolution in 1917 anarchist movements declined in most places and revolutionary Communists took the place of anarchists as *the* bogeymen to be discovered in every corner. More recently new currents of rebellion have arisen to which it is difficult to attach the "Communist" label, and the dread specter of anarchism has been called to service again.

As the last selection in this volume argues, there is reason to perceive anarchism in the contempory situation. This is not to say that the exorcisers of political devils are right in their accusations and fear-mongering: both anarchists and Communists have rarely been what, or even *who*, their enemies said they were. Dangers they may have been, but this is one area where the admonition "Know thine enemy" most often results only in the collection of distortions and falsehoods.

In most respects, anarchists have been ordinary men, not devils. If anything has distinguished them from others it has not been "evil" character, but an extraordinary passion for what they regard as justice.

They have, however, without exception been rebels. A spirit of rebellion against the established order of society is the single most distinctive quality of anarchist convictions, and one of the few that all share. The rebellion may be purely philosophical, it may seek change in the existing order by pacific means, or it may be acted out through violent agitation and revolution. The rebellious spirit is directed against all social conditions thought to be repressive: this usually means private property as well as government, and it means also a host of other institutions that many nonanarchists regard as essential constituents of a just and orderly society.

The anarchist assault on what others believe to be vital to their very existence makes anarchism intolerable. This is the substance behind past fears about anarchism. Repudiation of what seems sacred naturally excites the strongest and most unrelenting opposition, although the expression of opposition most often has been related only remotely to the reality of the anarchist "threat."

Rejection of anarchism also takes a more rational form, though a hardly less total one. "Suppose," it may be said, "that no *particular* institution or custom is sacrosanct; nevertheless, we must have an organized society, which requires govern-

ment, and other institutions as well. Anarchism is fundamentally antisocial because of its insistence on individual liberty. Any
philosophy which rejects society is irresponsible, impossible,
and unworthy of serious consideration."

Yet anarchism is anything but antisocial; indeed, for most
anarchists a concern for a just and integral society is more
primary than their concern for individual liberty. The distinc-
tiveness of their position results from their conviction that men
can be really social, and society truly real, only when individuals are really free—and this means ordering society not
through the dictates of power but through voluntary cooperation and self-imposed restraints.

To clarify this, let us go back to the first lines of this
introduction. There we cited one definition of "anarchy"—that
it signifies an absence of government and law. This, like the
statements immediately following, differs from an anarchist's
understanding of the matter. If one refers to the Greek origins
of the word, it is seen that anarchy denotes a condition where
"no one prevails"—that is, no one stands in a position of power
or authority over others.

Conventional political thought includes various assumptions
about the necessity for some such authority, so that a society
can be orderly and those who would disrupt it can be restrained. Hence, if "no one prevails" there will be no order and
evil-doers will inflict injury on those weaker than themselves,
resulting in violence and chaos.

Anarchists repudiate these assumptions and inferences,
maintaining that individuals are able to maintain social order
and justice without the intervention of external authority. This
they believe *can* be done by individual and joint voluntary
action, and *will* be done given the existence of certain vital
conditions. Thus they regard anarchy not as chaos but as the
only possible means of really ordering human affairs—
"government" in a sense, but self-government rather than the
government of some men by others.

More than that, anarchists insist that conventional government—no matter what its constitution and laws—*must* violate

the person and spirit of man. Both by its own violations and by sustaining such institutions as private property and authoritarian churches, government keeps society fragmented and at war with itself. It keeps citizens too repressed and impoverished, materially and spiritually, for them really to be *men,* much less social beings.

Thus, in the anarchist view, people are deluded when they suppose that order and justice are created and regulated by law and powerful institutions. Such order is mere appearance, behind which actually is the chaos of men struggling to subjugate and hurt each other, to gain at the expense of others. Such justice is a sham, called righteous by those able to dominate while making law serve their own interests. This is what Proudhon meant when he said that government is anarchy—the anarchy of disorder and the rule of force.

Outrage at this supposed state of affairs is the common denominator of anarchists, but besides those mentioned earlier there are few specifications of their beliefs that can be applied equally to all of them. Anarchism has always been a matter more of distinctive temper and relative degrees of emphasis than of specific defining convictions. While many anarchists may share a particular idea, few would agree with anyone else about a whole structure of ideas. Nevertheless, they have been able to form close bonds with each other, basing their collaboration upon a common spirit of outrage at injustice and of yearning for a better world. Lacking the agreement about doctrine and program that generally united men in comparable movements, anarchists have been more loosely knit and more dependent on sustaining a spirit itself closely tied to contemporary events.

Because there has been continuing change in the character of these events, and of ideas generally prevalent on the left which affect anarchism, the apparent character of anarchism has shifted. These changes, however, have been more in relative emphasis than anything else. The first anarchists were philosophers with no movements in which their ideas could be applied, and they gave more stress to individualism than was common later. Then revolutionary and labor movements began to develop in the mid-nineteenth century and afterward; anarchists became more action oriented, and more concerned with developing plans for a postrevolutionary society. (For an anarchist transitional between these first two stages, see the selections by Proudhon.)

As the movements grew in strength, so did the intensity of repressive efforts leveled against them by governments and employers. This struggle was prolonged and bitter, and both sides often initiated bloody violence. In this stage (see the selections by Berkman and Goldman) most anarchists were more preoccupied with the immediate struggle than with what might follow its successful conclusion; some had no use whatever for general theorizing. It was then that violent rhetoric and sometimes concomitant action were employed by a number of anarchists: destruction of supposed oppressors appeared to be the only possible or satisfying response to events.

When anarchists were no longer able to lead revolutionary mass movements, they again became more concerned with ideas, revising old concepts to fit changing conditions. Action tended to be confined to resisting authority while actively combating it only in limited ways, as in opposition to military conscription, and to developing projects that could both increase liberty and lead a few steps toward an anarchist future. (For this stage, see Wieck's essay.)

Most recently, anarchism has appeared in more widespread and active movements of rebellion. Like anarchists in mass movements half a century ago, the "new breed" often is more concerned with immediate action than with the details of what may happen later, and they are bitterly, sometimes violently, antagonistic toward established authorities. Most do not, however, adopt positions of pure anarchism, combining instead elements of its ideas and spirit with qualities and concepts of other radical movements. (Today's rebels are discussed in Goodman's article. For further historical details, see Novak's essay.)

Explaining this frequency of anarchist attitudes among contemporary rebels also says something about past differences between anarchism and other left-wing groups. The others, especially Marx and his followers, and anarchists often were deeply antagonistic toward each other, much more so than conflicts in ideas may seem to have required. To a large degree this was a matter of factional and personal rivalries and of the exclusiveness of parties insisting on adherence to a single ideology, but the issues dividing them ran deeper.

The key issue is how the new world is to be reached. Many socialists would concede that the state structure can ultimately be dismantled, reduced to administrative machinery with minimal functions. However, they attack anarchists for claiming that this can and must be done immediately.

Marxists have maintained that the dominant power of the oppressors—aristocrats and after them the bourgeoisie—can be ended solely by making the power of the oppressed still greater. The conflict is irreconcilable. A victorious people will in time eliminate the last vestiges and roots of power of the former ruling classes, doing so by eliminating class distinctions themselves. Only then will there no longer be a need for the state's authority. To reduce it any sooner would just permit the antisocial struggle between rich and poor to continue indefinitely. To Marxists, anarchism was a betrayal of the revolutionary cause—hence the sharpness of their antagonism.

Others less concerned with class struggle than conventional Marxists have further elaborated this type of criticism. Whether or not they regard a stateless society as a desirable final goal, they maintain that the instruments of governmental authority are necessary for reshaping society into the desired forms. Even without aggravated class conflict, resistance by many to change can be anticipated and must be overcome. A directive force is required to coordinate and organize the joint efforts needed to develop an economy of abundance, improved education, and other essential social conditions. Moreover, though men in a just society may restrain themselves from antisocial behavior, until such a society develops there will be a need for government regulation of behavior.

Many moderate socialists have maintained that the only moral path to the good society—and perhaps the only one actually practicable—is the normal process of democratic politics and legislation. By definition such an evolutionary series of reforms requires continuing governmental institutions; it also reflects a pragmatic, compromising temperament not compatible with the sharply rebellious spirit typical of anarchists.

In emphatically rejecting all such criticisms, anarchists reflect a very different conception of the nature of government. Others on the left have believed that the main objection to existing regimes and laws is the assertion that they are controlled by people of privilege; laws act mainly to protect this privilege, to the disadvantage of the masses. By the extension of democracy or, more radically, by the destruction of all middle and upper class power, government can be made the instrument of the people, acting in their service for good and necessary purposes.

Anarchists, however, insist that *any* imperative authority, even that of a popular socialist government or the joint decision of an egalitarian community, must violate individual liberty. Such violation must, in turn, prevent achieving justice and genuine community, a society undivided by internal antagonism and antisocial feeling and action.

They believe, moreover, that elements of irremediable corruption are inherent in any system of authority, even those ostensibly controlled by the masses. They do not want a revolution that merely replaces old power centers with new ones, for any power by its very nature will be tyrannical.

The reasons for this conviction are many; most are summed up in the notion that the State, no matter how constituted, is alien from most or all of the society it governs. It can not be the embodiment of the citizenry, but is instead an institution with needs, views, and goals peculiar to itself. Rather than expressing and enacting the needs and wishes of society's members, the State has a life of its own, and serves society as *it* sees fit, imposing its will on a largely helpless and often resentful population, and prevailing over it only through compulsion.

Leftists could treat such an argument skeptically when there were no socialist governments yet in being, and when they could regard existing democracies as mere shams, the instruments of the bourgeoisie. However, much additional experience with the deficiencies of "popular" regimes, including socialist ones, has made the argument seem more plausible. It is one of the reasons why anarchism is attractive to today's rebels, many of whom find government in nearly all known forms to be alien and hostile to their aspirations; it is difficult for them to conceive of the modern bureaucratic state as a vehicle for progress, whatever its constitution. Moreover, many of the other traditional socialist notions we have referred to also seem out of date to a new generation.

Nevertheless, these anarchist attacks on the State do not explain how we are to change without government direction. Anarchists here are indefinite, for they believe that we can not specify with any precision what forms society should ultimately assume, or the modes of transition. These must be decided upon by the men who themselves will live by them.

The basic anarchist vision is one of a society where all relationships are those of social and economic equals who act together in voluntary cooperation for mutual benefit. In terms of this vision it is not possible for people to be directed in learning how to live this way: they must learn the new life by making and living it themselves. Not only is government unneeded for the transition, by directing the change it would prevent its being realized.

This understanding of the matter also appeals to present-day rebels. When they speak of "creating new life styles," they only repeat an old attitude of anarchists.

Of course anarchists have not been alone in seeking to increase and protect individual liberty, nor in efforts to achieve social progress. They differ from others by insisting both that such goals can be gained only through social revolution and that government is not compatible with these goals.

The nonleftist theoretician desiring these objectives does not think social revolution is the only reason for rejecting anarchism. Usually it is maintained that for men to live in society there must be restraint of those natural impulses and passions that lead to injurious acts, and some limitation upon the pursuit of self-interest, where one's desires or interests conflict with those of others. For the needed restraints to be maintained, institutionalized authority is required. Otherwise men will not adhere to restraints with sufficient regularity, if at all, and will not even agree on what the restraints should be.

Therefore, government (and other institutions) are essential to make the rules defining the restraints and to make sure that the rules are followed. Such institutions are further required to gather the joint force and capacities of society for the accomplishment of common purposes, such as public works construction or military defense. Even though all may desire that these purposes be achieved, the authority of leadership and law are necessary to direct people in these common affairs, or their various contributions will not be coordinated.

An anarchist will contend that to tell a man what he must and must not do is necessarily to deny him liberty, and that he should be free to obey the dictates of his own will only. Critics would reply that it is not liberty which is demanded here, but *license*. License can only impinge on the rights of others and, when enjoyed by the foolish, headstrong, or immoral man, can even result in his self-destruction. True liberty is to be free to act as a just man, not merely as a willful one.

Few anarchists, however, maintain simply that individuals should be free to do whatever they will. Anarchists agree that individuals must act justly, not willfully, but insist that the restraints be self-imposed. They are convinced that restraints imposed by any sort of external authority must be coercive, repressive, and a negation of freedom.

Of such convictions one can say that they confuse the rule of justice under law with the abuse of authority often experienced by many. When men in power rule willfully, in the absence of or in disregard for law, or when the laws are wrongful, then government is tyrannical. But if the law is just and authorities act in accord with it, then men have nothing to fear from government. Rather than negating freedom, it creates it. If men are to be free, they must live by rational rules; otherwise they will be the slaves of their passions and the victims of the passions of others. Basing life upon the rules of right reason liberates men to exercise and develop their natural faculties to their fullest. Only in this way will social progress be achieved.

Critics of anarchism maintain that government is necessary to ensure the opportunity of all to live in this way, and to define the rules and teach them to those unable to formulate them alone. Laws with a sound basis in reason should be acceptable to all maturely rational men, who will obey them voluntarily and gladly. The purpose of political and legal science, and of reforms of government and law, is simply to perfect the rationalization of the system. Though it continues to be imperfect, there is no other way to universal justice, and anarchism merely gives up the effort in a folly of despair.

Anarchists, however, respond by saying that relatively little of the legal structure erected and enforced by governments can be applied with equal justice to all, or even with partial justice to most of us. The personalities, circumstances, and interests of different individuals are much too varied for legal determination of what is right and just to be universally valid.

An anarchist would agree that there are rules which can be universally applied because everyone accepts them, whether because they represent conventional beliefs and customary practices (or what people think to be universal truths), or because they are convenient or necessary for everyone. However, anarchists are convinced that such rules can not be translated with justice into laws which people will be compelled to obey. They can not be applied and enforced with sufficient flexibility to allow for human variability. (For example, homicide may always be wrong, but are all murders crimes of the same magnitude? If not, how do you define legally differences in degree of culpability when the circumstances vary as widely as they do in killings?) Universal rules there can be, but offenses against them have to be judged and corrective action taken as unique instances.

Anarchists would admit rather few such rules, relative to the number represented in present legal codes—and their resistance to these laws is not just objection to the imposition of uniformity on an infinitely variable humanity. They hold that most laws can be no more than instruments for maintaining a State structure, an economic order, and a social hierarchy which are fundamentally iniquitous, and are inimical to the basic objectives government should pursue: humane justice, social solidarity and tranquility, and the society's spiritual and material strength and growth.

Democratic government is intended to achieve impartiality and government in the interests of all through the participation of all in government. Anarchists believe that this ideal can not be fulfilled: those to whom the people's authority is delegated do not and can not act as their constituents require. Instead, representatives and officials act in their own interests, those of political parties, and those of privileged minorities with powers far in excess of ordinary people. Anarchists are cynical about the possibilities of officials acting disinterestedly; there is too much occasion for corruption by the prerogatives of power and by the methods needed to attain power. Even when relatively uncorrupted and impartial, those in authority are too distant from the bulk of the populace really to know their needs and beliefs. Moreover, in their demand for total self-government, anarchists deny that an individual can delegate to anyone else the right and responsibility to make decisions for himself— including those which require self-restraint in order that the interests of others may be served.

The State both prevents the exercise of human freedom and divides society into antagonistic fragments—but while anarchist attacks have focused on the State's repressive and divisive functions, they have also asserted that the same thing is accomplished by virtually the entire range of established economic, social, and religious institutions. Here the brunt of the anarchist critique can be seen shifting with particular historical circumstances. Originally the enemy of mankind was seen as a more or less coherent bloc of repressive institutions and social elements: government bureaucracies themselves; capitalist employers, managers, investors, financiers, and merchants; property owners and renters; elites of aristocrats, military officers, and upper-level officials; and churches—their hierarchies and their teachings.

Today, with the enormous growth in industrialized countries of huge, impersonal institutional structures—both public and private—anarchists see the "enemy of mankind" differently, and they have had to alter and broaden their critique. They have contended that in complex modern society repression has come to be much more than a matter of an alien State, restrictive laws, and subjugation of impoverished masses by bosses and landlords.

In an age when many more people than ever before have material security, anarchists believe that fulfillment of other, vital human needs is almost altogether wanting. In an age when governments are more benevolent to more people than ever before, and when they *seem* to be more democratic, anarchists have altered and added to their critiques of government, but maintain that its modern development has given added strength and urgency to their conclusions about it. In an age when churches are less powerful and more "progressive" then ever before, anarchists see in other institutions—public schools, universities, television, and the popular press, for example—much of the obfuscation of truth and hoodwinking of the people which were among their chief charges against organized religion. In an age where hereditary elites are less powerful than ever before, anarchists perceive more formidable new elites.

In the contemporary situation oppression is less a matter of the State and more of many relatively separate public agencies and private corporations, less of individual bosses, landlords, and tyrannizing officials and more of impersonal, depersonalizing institutions of great size and complexity. The barriers to "liberation" are less a matter of calculated maintenance of a repressive status quo than of a systematic inertia of institutions too unwieldy to be readily subject to significant modification. The interrelationship of these complex institutions is unclear, but that they are repressive seems clear not only to anarchists but to many others as well.

Thus it is that anarchism has assumed renewed relevance. The anarchist belief that men can live without government is difficult or impossible for most people to accept. Yet as long as we have such difficulty living *with* government, anarchism's relevance and potential appeal will continue to be felt.

In determining the selections for this volume, an attempt has been made to present essays representative of different types, styles, and periods of anarchist writing, rather than to include the full range of anarchist concerns and arguments, or samples of each of the major anarchist writers. The quantity of anarchist literature is too great to do otherwise. A number of possible selections were discarded because of ponderous style, unsuitable length, or because they are difficult to understand fully if one is not familiar with their original contexts.

The selection of essays critical of anarchism was made difficult by a paucity of useful works. Most critical writing has been little more than impassioned polemic, and much of the rest is seriously marred by the authors' ignorance of important aspects of anarchist theory. The best of the critical writing usually treats anarchists individually, without attempting an over-all evaluation of anarchist philosophy. There is very little general criticism of real merit; much of what does exist is represented here.

1
What Is Government?

PIERRE-JOSEPH
PROUDHON

P.-J. Proudhon (1809–1865) was one of the first modern anarchists, and probably was the most profound anarchist theoretician of all. His works are very lengthy and complex, however, and few have known or appreciated him as well as they have his successors. In this country he is particularly ill understood, in part because very little of his work has been translated into English, and that little is from his earlier and less important writings.

Oh, man in your individuality! Can it be that you have rotted in this baseness for sixty centuries? You call yourself pure and sacred, but you are only the whore, the sucker, the goat of your servants, your monks, and your mercenary soldiers. You know this and you endure it! To be GOVERNED is to be kept under surveillance, inspected, spied upon, bossed, law-ridden, regulated, penned in, indoctrinated, preached at, registered, evaluated, appraised, censured, ordered about, by creatures who have neither the right, nor the knowledge, nor the virtue to do so. To be GOVERNED is to be at each operation, at each transaction, at each movement, marked down, record-

Excerpt from *Idée générale de la révolution au XIXe siècle, Oeuvres Complètes de P.-J. Proudhon,* nouvelle édition (Paris: Riviere, 1924), p. 344. Translation by the editor and S. Valerie Hoffman. Complete English text. *General Idea of the Revolution in the Nineteenth Century,* trans. John Beverley Robinson (London: Freedom Press, 1923). This book was written in 1851.

ed, inventoried, priced, stamped, measured, numbered, assessed, licensed, authorized, sanctioned, endorsed, reprimanded, obstructed, reformed, rebuked, chastised. It is, under the pretense of public benefit and in the name of the general interest, to be requisitioned, drilled, fleeced, exploited, monopolized, extorted, squeezed, hoaxed, robbed; then at the slightest resistance, the first word of complaint, to be squelched, corrected, vilified, bullied, hounded, tormented, bludgeoned, disarmed, strangled, imprisoned, shot down, judged, condemned, deported, sacrificed, sold, betrayed, and to top it off, ridiculed, made a fool of, outraged, dishonored. That's government, that's its justice, that's its morality! And to think that there are democrats among us who claim that there is some good in government—socialists who support this infamy in the name of Liberty, Equality, and Fraternity—proletarians who proclaim their candidacy for the Presidency of the Republic! Hypocrisy!

2 *What Is Anarchism?*

ALEXANDER BERKMAN

Alexander Berkman (1870–1936), who immigrated from Russia as a youth, was one of the most outstanding anarchists in the United States during the movement's heyday in the late nineteenth and early twentieth centuries. He served fourteen years in prison for his unsuccessful attempt to assassinate the coal and steel baron, Henry Clay Frick, in revenge for the killing of workers by Pinkerton guards during the Homestead Strike, in 1892. Berkman and Emma Goldman (see pp. 34–49) were lifelong friends and co-workers.

I want to tell you about Anarchism.

I want to tell you what Anarchism is, because I think it is well you should know it. Also because so little is known about it, and what is known is generally hearsay and mostly false.

I want to tell you about it, because I believe that Anarchism is the finest and biggest thing man has ever thought of; the only thing that can give you liberty and well-being, and bring peace and joy to the world.

I want to tell you about it in such plain and simple language that there will be no misunderstanding it. Big words and high-sounding phrases serve only to confuse. Straight thinking means plain speaking.

But before I tell you what Anarchism is, I want to tell you what it *is not*.

From *Now and After: The ABC of Communist Anarchism* (New York: Vanguard Press, Inc., and the Jewish Anarchist Federation, 1929), pp. ix–xi.

That is necessary because so much falsehood has been spread about Anarchism. Even intelligent persons often have entirely wrong notions about it. Some people talk about Anarchism without knowing a thing about it. And some lie about Anarchism, because they don't want *you* to know the truth about it.

Anarchism has many enemies; they won't tell you the truth about it. Why Anarchism has enemies and who they are, you will see later, in the course of this story. Just now I can tell you that neither your political boss nor your employer, neither the capitalist nor the policeman, will speak to you honestly about Anarchism. Most of them know nothing about it, and all of them hate it. Their newspapers and publications—the capitalistic press—are also against it.

Even most Socialists and Bolsheviki misrepresent Anarchism. True, the majority of them don't know any better. But those who do know better also often lie about Anarchism and speak of it as "disorder and chaos." You can see for yourself how dishonest they are in this: the greatest teachers of Socialism—Karl Marx and Friedrich Engels—had taught that Anarchism would come from Socialism. They said that we must first have Socialism, but that after Socialism there will be Anarchism, and that it would be a freer and more beautiful condition of society to live in than Socialism. Yet the Socialists, who swear by Marx and Engels, insist on calling Anarchism "chaos and disorder," which shows you how ignorant or dishonest they are.

The Bolsheviki do the same, although their greatest teacher, Lenin, had said that Anarchism would follow Bolshevism, and that then it will be better and freer to live.

Therefore I must tell you, first of all, what Anarchism *is not.*

It is *not* bombs, disorder, or chaos.

It is *not* robbery and murder.

It is *not* a war of each against all.

It is *not* a return to barbarism or to the wild state of man.

Anarchism is the very opposite of all that.

Anarchism means that you should be free; that no one should enslave you, boss you, rob you, or impose upon you.

It means that you should be free to do the things you want to do; and that you should not be compelled to do what you don't want to do.

It means that you should have a chance to choose the kind of a life you want to live, and live it without anybody interfering.

It means that the next fellow should have the same freedom as you, that every one should have the same rights and liberties.

It means that all men are brothers, and that they should live like brothers, in peace and harmony.

That is to say, that there should be no war, no violence used by one set of men against another, no monopoly and no poverty, no oppression, no taking advantage of your fellow-man.

In short, Anarchism means a condition of society where all men and women are free, and where all enjoy equally the benefits of an ordered and sensible life.

"Can that be?" you ask; "and how?"

"Not before we all become angels," your friend remarks.

Well, let us talk it over. Maybe I can show you that we can be decent and live as decent folks even without growing wings.

3 The Place of Anarchism in the History of Political Thought

DERRY NOVAK

Derry Novak (1919—) is an associate professor of political science at McMaster University in Hamilton, Ontario. His approach is that of an objective scholar with a fondness for philosophical anarchism. A number of men developed ideas akin to anarchism before the nineteenth century; the subject is an interesting one and is discussed by Novak, but this section of his article is omitted here. Additional historical comment will be found in the selection by James Joll.

Anarchism is one of those concepts about which there generally is deep ignorance or profound misunderstanding.

"In the popular mind," says Bertrand Russell, "an Anarchist is a person who throws bombs and commits other outrages, either because he is more or less insane, or because he uses the pretense of extreme political opinions as a cloak for criminal proclivities."[1] Yet in the history of political thought, as well as in the history of social movements, anarchism has played a role which cannot be overlooked.

Anarchism is not only a political theory in the narrow meaning of the term, but also a social theory understood in the broad sense. As such a theory, anarchism—since it is con-

From *The Review of Politics*, July 1958, pp. 307–313, 320–329. A part of the text and most of the notes are omitted.

cerned with the problems of power, authority, and coercion, especially as manifested in the machinery of the State, and since it strives to show how the exercise of power of man over man, together with the institutions through which it is carried out, should be eradicated—necessarily deals with the complex problems of both national and international politics. Anarchism, however, while paying attention to the individual as a citizen of the State, is interested in him also as a human being, as a member of various groups of human beings, and as a member of the human race. Thus in the consideration of the problems of men, whether a given problem be conceived narrowly or broadly, in the relation of man to man, of one citizen to another, of a citizen to the State, or in the relation of State with State, and whether it be conceived in economic, political, social, or ethical terms, anarchism as a social philosophy will be found to express a judgment.

Like many other political and social theories, anarchism starts from premises based on the appraisal of human nature, from which it draws its conclusions concerning the right kind of social organization. Unlike other reformist and revolutionary theories, however, anarchism much more readily and determinedly refutes or supplements the accepted tenets of other theories and develops new principles and interpretations, always questioning the very foundations of social institutions, both those existing and those envisaged by other reformers and revolutionaries.

Peter Kropotkin defined anarchism as a "principle or theory of life and conduct under which society is conceived without government . . . harmony in such a society being obtained, not by submission to law, or by obedience to authority, but by free agreements concluded between various groups, territorial and professional, freely constituted for the sake of production and consumption, as also for the satisfaction of the infinite variety of needs and aspirations of a civilized being."[2] Oscar Jászi points out that "Anarchism covers so many distinct conceptions and tendencies that it is difficult to reduce them all to a common denominator," and considers anarchism not so much a social theory as "a mass ideology colored by many emotional and religious elements."[3] In this approach Jászi comes close to Zenker, who considers both anarchism and socialism "forms of idolatry" with different idols, "religions and not sciences, dogmas and not speculations," and kinds of "honestly meant social mysticism" which strive for "the establishment of a terrestrial Eden, of a land of the absolute Ideal, whether it be Freedom or Equality."[4] Jászi, by drawing attention to the variety of conceptions and tendencies covered by the term "anarchism," also comes close to Paul Eltzbacher in his judgment of anarchism.[5] With these provisions in mind, however, Jászi thinks that anarchism can be defined as "an attempt to establish justice (that is, equality and reciprocity) in all human relations by the complete elimination of the state (or by a genuine minimization of its activity) and its replacement by an entirely free and spontaneous co-operation among individuals, groups, regions, and nations." . . .

One need not go so far as the anarchist writer who said that "there are as many variations of Anarchism as there are Anarchists," but one cannot fail to realize that the differences between various anarchist theories and theorists, as well as the emphasis laid upon the right to differ, are part of the nature of anarchism. In the sphere of anarchism as a political movement, this attitude is reflected in the looseness of groups, which cannot be considered organizations on the pattern of political parties, and which lack accepted leadership and discipline. It can also be noted in the lack of a general program to which all members have to subscribe, and in the freedom left to individual members to advocate views and measures that may be in conflict with those of the majority.

In spite of the differences, there are certain underlying features which are common to all anarchist trends. These features stand out in the several definitions of anarchism given above and are contained in most other definitions of anarchism or in treatises on it. The rejection of the State, listed by Eltzbacher, is one feature, but it is not the only one common to the various anarchist trends. Even, if looked upon as a basic principle of anarchism, implied in the very word, the rejection of the State can still be looked upon as following from another principle, namely, the acknowledgment and assertion of the independent value of the individual and his right to a free and full development. The essence of anarchist thought is the emphasis on the freedom of the individual, leading to the denial and condemnation of any authority which hinders his free and full development, particularly the State. The rejection of all authority represents the main contribution of anarchism to political thought and distinguishes it from other political and social theories, some of which, for example, liberalism, may have other features similar to anarchism, and may even start from the same basis. Bound up with these fundamental ideas are the theories and criticisms of law and government, of property, of the whole social and economic system and patterns of behavior prevalent in it, and of the ways and means suggested or preached as remedies or panaceas for the evils. Underlying all these thoughts and constantly present in them, whether explicitly or implicitly, are views of human nature. It may, then, be suggested that the various anarchist trends have in common a belief in individual freedom and a denial of authority, especially in the form of the State. In the development of these fundamental ideas, however, there are differences among anarchists relating to the questions of government, law, property, social and economic institutions, revolutions, and so on. They also—and this, at first sight, may seem incongruous—have varying views on human nature.

Anarchism as a social ideology is really a modern phenomenon. To use an analogy, it may be said that anarchism is like a tree which attained its full development in the nineteenth century, while some of its roots were firmly implanted in the eighteenth, and some of its branches have reached into the twentieth century. Although this is true of anarchism as an ideology, the revolt against the subjugation of the individual by authority and the struggle for the assertion of the individual's rights to unfettered development and self-expression are probably as old as the existence of authoritarian and coercive institutions, and the ideas emphasizing the value of individual free-dom and denouncing its restrictions by authority have been voiced by thinkers through the ages. Kropotkin actually sees a libertarian, anti-authoritarian tendency—the tendency of mu-tual aid—as an important evolutionary and historical factor. According to him, this tendency finds expression in the direct action of popular masses when they create organizations in defense of their rights against the encroachments of conquerors and powerful minorities, such as clans, village communities, guilds, and medieval cities. Although anthropologists and histo-rians would not agree with Kropotkin's thesis in its entirety, owing to its emphasis on selected factors, his analysis neverthe-less suggests a trend which every social science must study and which in modern times both individual and social psychology attempt to analyze and explain.

Some writers on anarchism have attempted to trace anarchist ideas in thinkers and movements of the Western world from ancient times. One may not accept many claims made by these writers but, particularly in view of the largely critical and negative attitude of anarchism to social arrangements, one must be prepared to encounter anarchist traits in different, and sometimes even contradictory, ideas and systems of thought. Thus, as in the case of liberalism or socialism, it can be seen that views akin to anarchism, and sometimes clearly anarchist, have been formed in the West from the times of the ancient Greeks to the nineteenth century in both the secular and religious spheres. . . .

With the publication, in 1793, of William Godwin's *An Enquiry Concerning Political Justice and Its Influence on General Virtue and Happiness,* there began a systematic elabo-ration and formulation of modern anarchist thought, based upon a comprehensive analysis of the economic, political and social factors, as well as upon scientific, ethical and philosoph-ical thought. This elaboration and presentation was effected, after Godwin, chiefly by Proudhon, Bakunin, Stirner, Tucker, Tolstoy, and Kropotkin. Other anarchist writers, for instance, Elisée Reclus, Errico Malatesta, Jean Grave, Domela

Nieuwenhuis, A. Hamon, Max Nettlau, Emma Goldman, Alexander Berkman, and others, draw mainly on their work. Apart from Tolstoy's religious anarchism, the theorists of anarchism adhere mostly to anarcho-communism, and some also to anarcho-syndicalism and anarcho-individualism.

Since the latter part of the last century anarchism has taken predominantly the anarcho-communistic form advocated by Peter Kropotkin (1842–1921),[6] whose ideas are in many respects related to those of William Godwin (1756–1836), Pierre-Joseph Proudhon (1809–1865),[7] probably the first man to call himself an anarchist, and Michael Bakunin (1814–1876).[8] The term "anarchist communism" was coined by Peter Kropotkin who first advocated its use at an international anarchist congress in Switzerland in 1880, believing that it conveyed the idea of unity or harmony between individual freedom and a "well-ordered" social life. Anarchist communism views the individual as essentially a social being who can achieve full development only in society, while society can benefit only when its members are free. Individual and social interests are not contradictory but complementary and would attain their natural harmony if authoritarian social institutions, particularly the State, established to create and perpetuate the privileges of some at the expense of others, did not interfere.

Anarcho-syndicalism lays emphasis on the economic as opposed to the political struggle of the working class. It believes that the trade unions, or syndicates, can serve both as leading units in the present-day struggle for the amelioration of the conditions of the workers, and as the bases of a new economic organization of society after a victorious revolution, in which the General Strike is to play the leading part. The anarcho-syndicalists intend to abolish the State and carry on the activities of society through the syndicates, associated by industries and localities. Syndicalism has been an important part of the working class movement in France, especially since the congress in Limoges in 1895, and before the Civil War in Spain in 1936–1939 the anarcho-syndicalist movement was also strong in that country. Anarcho-syndicalism has produced no out-

standing theoretician of its own, and its principles are sometimes accepted by anarcho-communists in their approach to the
economic problems of society.

The two outstanding representatives of anarchist individualism are Max Stirner (1806–1856) in Germany and Benjamin
Tucker (1854–1939) in the United States of America. Stirner
developed his views in *Der Einzige und sein Eigentum,* published in Leipzig in 1845. The core of his message was the
proclamation of the absolute freedom of the individual. The
individual has the right to do whatever he wants, and everything that would curtail his freedom must be fought against.
Stirner is not only against the State, the law and private
property, but also against many concepts, such as God, country, family, and love, because they claim the individual's alle-
giance and thus limit his freedom. He did not condemn all
ideals as useless, but emphasized that they should be pursued
for purely egoistic reasons, for the pleasure and happiness of
the individual, and not because they were a duty. He advocated an "association of egoists," which individuals could freely
enter to pursue their particular interests, and leave when and
as they pleased. Men should undergo an inward change, come
to the realization of their own individuality and their own
good, and by a violent insurrection overthrow the existing
system.

Tucker started with the assumption that every man had the
right to oppress other men, provided he had the power to do
so. The life of the individual, however, being intimately linked
with that of society, it is in the pure self-interest of every
individual to grant equal liberty to others. "Mind your own
business!" then becomes the moral law of the anarchist. The
State interferes with the freedom of the individual and therefore should be abolished, but property in the products of one's
own labor is justified. Tucker also admitted the usefulness of a
flexible law, which should be applied by jury, particularly in
cases of violation of personal liberty and of contract. He advocated peaceful spreading of the anarchist ideas by the printed

and spoken word to convince a sufficient number of people of the advantages of anarchism, which would then be gradually established.[9]

The religious anarchism of Leo Tolstoy (1828–1910) follows from his interpretation of the teachings of Christ. . . . Tolstoy emphasizes that it is the teaching of love which is the "fundamental essence of the soul." Only by substituting the law of man for the law of God do men justify violence, oppression, inequality. By following the law of God, men will love, help, and forgive one another, and live in peace and harmony without having any use for government, man-made laws, courts, police, armies, prisons, and private property. While living in a corrupted world, the Christians should support neither the State nor the Church and offer passive resistance to them. Tolstoy believes that simple agricultural life best suits human nature and urges return to such a life.[10]

It may be noted that among our contemporaries the members of the Russian sect of the "Christians of the Universal Brotherhood," better known as the Doukhobors, adhere to and follow several principles held by Tolstoy, such as disobedience of governmental authorities in certain matters of conscience, rejection of an official Church, pacifism, agricultural life.

The affinity of anarchism with liberalism has already been noted in this essay. Like liberalism, anarchism bases its social philosophy on the considerations of the value of the individual in terms of his freedom, happiness, and prosperity. The same belief that, if individuals are left to pursue their natural desires, general benefit will be the result, is present in anarchism as in early liberalism. However, while the liberal doctrine has been qualified by the admission that some social authority is necessary to lead the "invisible hand" and see to it that the "natural" laws are not tampered with, anarchism refuses to accept such an admission. It still insists on applying the liberal idea of freedom in both the economic and political fields and it extends the liberal plea for a minimum of government to a complete negation of government: "When Jefferson clothes the basic concept of Liberalism in the words, 'That government is best which governs least,' then Anarchists say with Thoreau: 'That government is best which governs not at all.' "[11] The anarchist deny the necessity of government because of their belief—which most non-anarchists will dismiss as utopian—that the dictates of reason, or the social instincts of human nature, or both, if unhampered by external coercion, will secure free, harmonious social life. Such a life, moreover, will not display the inequalities which the liberals accept as a matter of fact, but will result in conditions of equality, reflected in socialistic or communistic arrangements.

Some writers on the political theory of anarchism, however, while accepting its kinship to liberalism, deny that anarchism is related to socialism either as a closely allied doctrine or as a branch of the general socialist theory, and indeed put anarchism and socialism as antitheses. Such judgment arises out of the conception of anarchism as a doctrine championing the rights of the individual against the rights of society, whereas socialism is conceived as a doctrine emphasizing the rights of society against those of the individual. Although this distinction may seem acceptable at first sight, further considerations upset it. Even the individualist anarchists reach conclusions which bring them close to socialists, and the anarchist communists, as the name implies, by trying to reach a synthesis and harmony of the individual and communal, or social, tendencies of human nature, are again necessarily brought close to socialists.

Socialism aims at a new society based on the common ownership of all, or a considerable proportion of, the means of production and distribution, in order to create a state in which every individual will receive from society all he needs for the development of his capacities, and in return will contribute, according to his powers, to the benefit of other members of society. This is also the aim of anarchism, particularly the anarchist communism which is now practically the only anarchist trend. It is often forgotten that the aim of socialism is to secure for man the greatest happiness and freedom compatible with the equal claims of others. This is also the goal of anarchism, and it was one of Kropotkin's merits that he paid much attention to the problem of reconciling the individualistic and social proclivities in man.

Like socialism in general, anarchism is opposed to private ownership of land and capital. Bertrand Russell actually stresses their relation in this respect and says that both arose "from the perception that private capital is a source of tyranny by certain individuals over others."[12] Socialism and anarchism differ in their professed aims. Even in this respect, however, the differences are not such as to violate their basic affinity: in its view of the ultimate "withering away" of the State Marxian socialism is closer to anarchism than to democratic socialism, while in their advocacy of the means for the transformation of society some anarchists, like the Marxists, preach violent revolution, and others, like the democratic socialists, advocate peaceful means. The advocacy and practice of individual terrorism by some anarchists, in particular toward the end of the last century, estranged them from the socialists, but terrorism was not condoned by the anarchist movement as a whole, and as a phenomenon arising out of extreme individualism and oppressive social and political conditions it has not been confined to the anarchists alone.

In the last century the anarchists considered themselves part of the socialist movement and were members of the International Working Men's Association until their split with the Marxists at the Hague Congress of the International in 1872. According to Kropotkin, they were at first called federalists, anti-authoritarians and anti-statists, but later their antagonists began to call them anarchists, using the word in a derogatory sense to denounce them as people set on causing disorder and chaos without contemplating the consequences of their actions. The anarchists themselves came to accept this designation, insisting at first on the word being written "an-archist," as Proudhon did in 1840, to denote that the term did not mean disorder but opposition to power. Gradually the word accepted in its present form.

A. Hamon, attempting to determine the psychological characteristics of an anarchist by arranging and analyzing the answers given to questions by numbers of anarchists from various countries, came to the conclusion that the basic psychological traits of an anarchist were rebelliousness, love of freedom, self-love or individualism, love of one's neighbors or altruism, sensitiveness, sense of justice, sense of logic, desire for knowledge, and proselytism. These characteristics could very well be found to be typical of most socialists and humanitarians. Hamon actually speaks of an "anarchist-socialist," and admits that these psychological traits can be found among other anarchists.

In this connection it is interesting to note that *Le Révolté*, the organ of the anarchist Jurasian Federation, which Kropotkin edited in Geneva, had, from its inception on February 22, 1879, until March 2, 1884, been designated as a "socialist organ," then two numbers appeared with the designation "anarchist organ," and only after that was the expression "communist-anarchist organ" used. Similarly, *Freedom,* started with Kropotkin's help in London in October 1886, began as a "journal of anarchist socialism," and only in June 1889, was the expression "anarchist communism" used. In his writings Kropotkin considered anarchism a branch of socialism, referring to it, for example, as one of the schools of socialism, or as the left wing of socialism. This stand, taken by Kropotkin and reflecting the general attitude of his time, is accepted by most writers on political theories of socialism and anarchism.

Modern anarchism, in common with all modern social theories, rejects any suggestions of being utopian. It claims that its conceptions are derived from the analysis of tendencies which are at work in society and that its philosophical and ethical ideas are based on scientific notions, as far as these can be obtained in the study of man. Besides its appeal to science, it also points to the anarchist influence in modern art, literature and philosophy, citing as illustrations the names of John Stuart Mill, Spencer, Guyau, Fouillé, Lessing, Fichte, Nietzsche, Wagner, Emerson, Whitman, Zola, Ibsen, and others. Seen as a whole, modern anarchism represents a socialist trend which lays emphasis on individual liberty and social justice, and

questions and revolts against everything that tends to produce
and worship authority, regimentation, and uniformity.

The kinship of anarchism with socialism helps to explain
both its relative strength in the second half of the last century
and its decline in the present. Together with other branches of
socialist thought in the last century, anarchism was a protest
against the evils of the growing industrial society—poverty,
disease, ignorance, oppression—and a reaffirmation of the hu-
manitarian principles of freedom, equality, and justice. At a
time when the State excluded vast numbers of people from the
rights of citizenship, it was not difficult for many to accept the
anarchist criticisms directed against it. However, as the
economic, social, and cultural conditions of the people gradually improved, and as the exercise of political power broadened,
it became clear that anarchism misjudged the nature of social
forces, in particular the nature and potentialities of political
power, and inevitably declined.

Having assumed that the State, since it arose as a means of
oppression of many by a few, must always be used for the
same purpose, the anarchists denied *a priori* any possibility of
changing the nature of the State. This genetic fallacy, as the
logicians would call it, led them to argue against other socialists
on the question of the State and to minimize or decry improvements gained through political means. Most of those who might
otherwise have seen some attraction in the anarchist arguments
were led to reject them, and supported the democratic socialists
who advocated the necessity of effecting the desired social
changes through the machinery of the State. The impact of this
situation was reflected even among the West European
Marxists who were accepting parliamentary government, rather
than revolution, as a means of political struggle. Moreover,
since the working class was gaining benefits through the State,
it tended to look upon the economic struggle as a supplement
to, and not the replacement of, the political struggle, as the
anarchists urged it to do, and thus even in the syndicates and
trade unions the anarchists were losing their influence. Much of

what they said appeared unrealistic and utopian. Acts of individual terrorism, committed by some anarchists, especially toward the end of the last century, expressed their impatience and frustration, born of impotence and inability to face and solve social problems, and alienated even those who might otherwise have been sympathetic.

Historical development has proceeded in a direction different from that expected by the anarchists. The great importance today of what we have come to know as the "welfare State" reflects the profound differences between the present concept of the nature and functions of the State and the *laissez faire* concept. Indeed, it may be suggested that in some significant respects we are adopting again the Aristotelian view of the State, and developing it further. As an uncompromising opponent of the State, and as a champion of small groups and conglomerations—political, economic, cultural, social—anarchism was compatible only with a less complex, and therefore more primitive, economic, political, and social structure of society. Consequently, its influence in the industrial countries of the West in the present century has declined to infinitesimal proportions. However, as a libertarian philosophy, anarchism cannot be dismissed as unimportant, particularly in the field of social and political ethics. It is still of intellectual significance, presenting a challenge to our thought and making us re-examine our views.

NOTES

1. Bertrand Russell, *Roads to Freedom: Socialism, Anarchism, and Syndicalism* (London, 1918), p. 49.
2. P. Kropotkin, "Anarchism," *Encyclopaedia Britannica* (1947), I, 873.
3. O. Jászi, "Anarchism," *Encyclopaedia of the Social Sciences* (1942), II, 46.
4. E. V. Zenker, *Anarchism: A Criticism and History of the Anarchist Theory* (London, 1898), p. 4.
5. See P. Eltzbacher, *Anarchism* (New York, London, 1908), especially chaps. X, XI, and the Conclusion.

6. See especially his *Anarchist Communism: Its Basis and Principles* (London, 1891); *Anarchist Morality* (London, 1892); *Les Temps Nouveaux* (Paris, 1894); *L'Anarchie, sa philosophie, son idéal* (Paris, 1896); *The State: Its Historic Role* (London, 1898); *Mutual Aid* (London, 1902); *The Conquest of Bread* (London, 1906); *Modern Science and Anarchism* (London, 1912); *Communisme et anarchie* (Paris, 1913); *Ethics* (New York, 1924).

7. For Proudhon, see his *Qu' est-ce que la propriété?* (Paris, 1840); *Système des contradictions économiques ou philosophie de la misère* (Paris, 1846); *La Solution du problème sociale* (Paris, 1848); *L'Idée générale de la Révolution au XIXè siecle* (Paris, 1851); *De la Justice dans la Révolution et dans l'Eglise*, 3 vols. (Paris, 1858); *Du principe fédératif* (Paris, 1863).

8. On Bakunin consult his *Oeuvres*, 6 vols. (Paris, 1895–1913); *God and State*, trans. by Benjamin Tucker, Preface by Carlo Cafiero and Elisée Reclus (Boston, 1893); *La Commune de Paris et la notion de l'Etat* (Paris, 1899); M. Dragomanov (ed.), *Michail Bakunins Socialpolitischer Briefwechsel mit Alexander Iw. Herzen und Ogarjow* (Stuttgart, 1895); G. P. Maksimov (ed.), *The Political Philosophy of Bakunin: Scientific Anarchism*, Preface by Bert F. Hoselitz, Introd. By Rudolf Rocker, Biographical Sketch by Max Nettlau (Glencoe, Ill., 1953).

9. Tucker's views appear in a selection of his articles, *Instead of a Book, by a Man too Busy to Write One: A Fragmentary Exposition of Philosophical Anarchism* (New York, 1893).

10. Out of the many books and pamphlets written by Tolstoy, for the basic statement of his philosophy see *The Kingdom of God Is within You; What I Believe (My Religion)* (London, n.d.); *L'Eglise et l'Etat*, trad. par J. W. Bienstock (Paris, 1905); *The Russian Revolution* (London, 1907?).

11. R. Rocker, *Anarcho-Syndicalism* (London, 1938), p. 23.

12. Russell, *op. cit.*, p. 52.

4 Anarchism: What It Really Stands For

EMMA GOLDMAN

Emma Goldman (1869–1940), like her friend Berkman an immigrant from Russia, was still more talented, fiery, and dynamic than he. She fought passionately for many unpopular causes in addition to anarchism, and deserves a major place in the tradition of American radicalism. With Berkman she produced Mother Earth *(1906–1918), one of the liveliest and best of American radical periodicals. In 1917 they were imprisoned for urging people to refuse cooperation with the wartime draft. After two years in jail they were deported to Europe, where they remained active in the cause of anarchism.*

ANARCHY

Ever reviled, accursed, ne'er understood,
    Thou art the grisly terror of our age.
"Wreck of all order," cry the multitude,
    "Art thou, and war and murder's endless rage."
O, let them cry. To them that ne'er have striven
    The truth that lies behind a word to find,
To them the word's right meaning was not given.
    They shall continue blind among the blind.
But thou, O word, so clear, so strong, so pure,
    Thou sayest all which I for goal have taken.
I give thee to the future! Thine secure
    When each at least unto himself shall waken.
Comes it in sunshine? In the tempest's thrill?
    I cannot tell—but it the earth shall see!
I am an Anarchist! Wherefore I will
    Not rule, and also ruled I will not be!

                   JOHN HENRY MACKAY

From *Anarchism and Other Essays* (New York: Mother Earth Publishing Association, 1911), pp. 53–73.

The history of human growth and development is at the same time the history of the terrible struggle of every new idea heralding the approach of a brighter dawn. In its tenacious hold on tradition, the Old has never hesitated to make use of the foulest and cruelest means to stay the advent of the New, in whatever form or period the latter may have asserted itself. Nor need we retrace our steps into the distant past to realize the enormity of opposition, difficulties, and hardships placed in the path of every progressive idea. The rack, the thumbscrew, and the knout are still with us; so are the convict's garb and the social wrath, all conspiring against the spirit that is serenely marching on.

Anarchism could not hope to escape the fate of all other ideas of innovation. Indeed, as the most revolutionary and uncompromising innovator, Anarchism must needs meet with the combined ignorance and venom of the world it aims to reconstruct.

To deal even remotely with all that is being said and done against Anarchism would necessitate the writing of a whole volume. I shall therefore meet only two of the principal objections. In so doing, I shall attempt to elucidate what Anarchism really stands for.

The strange phenomenon of the opposition to Anarchism is that it brings to light the relation between so-called intelligence and ignorance. And yet this is not so very strange when we consider the relativity of all things. The ignorant mass has in its favor that it makes no pretense of knowledge or tolerance. Acting, as it always does, by mere impulse, its reasons are like those of a child. "Why?" "Because." Yet the opposition of the uneducated to Anarchism deserves the same consideration as that of the intelligent man.

What, then, are the objections? First, Anarchism is impractical, though a beautiful ideal. Second, Anarchism stands for violence and destruction, hence it must be repudiated as vile and dangerous. Both the intelligent man and the ignorant mass judge not from a thorough knowledge of the subject, but either from hearsay or false interpretation.

A practical scheme, says Oscar Wilde, is either one already in existence, or a scheme that could be carried out under the existing conditions; but it is exactly the existing conditions that one objects to, and any scheme that could accept these conditions is wrong and foolish. The true criterion of the practical, therefore, is not whether the latter can keep intact the wrong or foolish; rather is it whether the scheme has vitality enough to leave the stagnant waters of the old, and build, as well as sustain, new life. In the light of this conception, Anarchism is indeed practical. More than any other idea, it is helping to do away with the wrong and foolish; more than any other idea, it is building and sustaining new life.

The emotions of the ignorant man are continuously kept at a pitch by the most blood-curdling stories about Anarchism. Not a thing too outrageous to be employed against this philosophy and its exponents. Therefore Anarchism represents to the unthinking what the proverbial bad man does to the child—a black monster bent on swallowing everything; in short, destruction and violence.

Destruction and violence! How is the ordinary man to know that the most violent element in society is ignorance; that its power of destruction is the very thing Anarchism is combating? Nor is he aware that Anarchism, whose roots, as it were, are part of nature's forces, destroys, not healthful tissue, but parasitic growths that feed on the life's essence of society. It is merely clearing the soil from weeds and sagebrush, that it may eventually bear healthy fruit.

Someone has said that it requires less mental effort to condemn than to think. The widespread mental indolence, so prevalent in society, proves this to be only too true. Rather than to go to the bottom of any given idea, to examine into its origin and meaning, most people will either condemn it altogether, or rely on some superficial or prejudicial definition of non essentials.

Anarchism urges man to think, to investigate, to analyze every proposition; but that the brain capacity of the average

reader be not taxed too much, I also shall begin with a definition, and then elaborate on the latter.

ANARCHISM: The philosophy of a new social order based on
liberty unrestricted by man-made law; the theory that all forms
of government rest on violence, and are therefore wrong and
harmful, as well as unnecessary.

The new social order rests, of course, on the materialistic
basis of life; but while all Anarchists agree that the main evil
today is an economic one, they maintain that the solution of
that evil can be brought about only through the consideration
of *every phase* of life—individual, as well as the collective; the
internal, as well as the external phases.

A thorough perusal of the history of human development
will disclose two elements in bitter conflict with each other;
elements that are only now beginning to be understood, not as
foreign to each other, but as closely related and truly harmonious, if only placed in proper environment: the individual and
social instincts. The individual and society have waged a re-
lentless and bloody battle for ages, each striving for supremacy
because each was blind to the value and importance of the
other. The individual and social instincts—the one a most
potent factor for individual endeavor, for growth, aspiration,
self-realization; the other an equally potent factor for mutual
helpfulness and social well-being.

The explanation of the storm raging within the individual,
and between him and his surroundings, is not far to seek. The
primitive man, unable to understand his being, much less the
unity of all life, felt himself absolutely dependent on blind,
hidden forces ever ready to mock and taunt him. Out of that
attitude grew the religious concepts of man as a mere speck of
dust dependent on superior powers on high, who can only be
appeased by complete surrender. All the early sagas rest on
that idea, which continues to be the *leitmotiv* of the biblical
tales dealing with the relation of man to God, to the State, to
society. Again and again the same motif, *man is nothing, the*

powers are everything. Thus Jehovah would only endure man on condition of complete surrender. Man can have all the glories of the earth, but he must not become conscious of himself. The State, society, and moral laws all sing the same refrain: Man can have all the glories of the earth, but he must not become conscious of himself.

Anarchism is the only philosophy which brings to man the consciousness of himself; which maintains that God, the State, and society are nonexistent, that their promises are null and void, since they can be fulfilled only through man's subordination. Anarchism is therefore the teacher of the unity of life; not merely in nature, but in man. There is no conflict between the individual and the social instincts, any more than there is between the heart and the lungs: the one the receptacle of a precious life essence, the other the repository of the element that keeps the essence pure and strong. The individual is the heart of society, conserving the essence of social life; society is the lungs which are distributing the element to keep the life essence—that is, the individual—pure and strong.

"The one thing of value in the world," says Emerson, "is the active soul; this every man contains within him. The soul active sees absolute truth and utters truth and creates." In other words, the individual instinct is the thing of value in the world. It is the true soul that sees and creates the truth alive, out of which is to come a still greater truth, the reborn social soul.

Anarchism is the great liberator of man from the phantoms that have held him captive; it is the arbiter and pacifier of the two forces for individual and social harmony. To accomplish that unity, Anarchism has declared war on the pernicious influences which have so far prevented the harmonious blending of individual and social instincts, the individual and society.

Religion, the dominion of the human mind; Property, the dominion of human needs; and Government, the dominion of human conduct, represent the stronghold of man's enslavement and all the horrors it entails. Religion! How it dominates man's mind, how it humiliates and degrades his soul. God is everything, man is nothing, says religion. But out of that nothing God has created a kingdom so despotic, so tyrannical, so cruel, so terribly exacting that naught but gloom and tears and blood have ruled the world since gods began. Anarchism rouses man to rebellion against this black monster. Break your mental fetters, says Anarchism to man, for not until you think and judge for yourself will you get rid of the dominion of darkness, the greatest obstacle to all progress.

Property, the dominion of man's needs, the denial of the right to satisfy his needs. Time was when property claimed a divine right, when it came to man with the same refrain, even as religion, "Sacrifice! Abnegate! Submit!" The spirit of Anarchism has lifted man from his prostrate position. He now stands erect, with his face toward the light. He has learned to see the insatiable, devouring, devastating nature of property, and he is preparing to strike the monster dead.

"Property is robbery," said the great French Anarchist Proudhon. Yes, but without risk and danger to the robber. Monopolizing the accumulated efforts of man, property has robbed him of his birthright, and has turned him loose a pauper and an outcast. Property has not even the time-worn excuse that man does not create enough to satisfy all needs. The A B C student of economics knows that the productivity of labor within the last few decades far exceeds normal demand. But what are normal demands to an abnormal institution? The only demand that property recognizes is its own gluttonous appetite for greater wealth, because wealth means power; the power to subdue, to crush, to exploit, the power to enslave, to outrage, to degrade. America is particularly boastful of her great power, her enormous national wealth. Poor America, of what avail is all her wealth, if the individuals comprising the nation are wretchedly poor? If they live in squalor, in filth, in crime, with hope and joy gone, a homeless, soilless army of human prey.

It is generally conceded that unless the returns of any business venture exceed the cost, bankruptcy is inevitable. But those engaged in the business of producing wealth have not yet

learned even this simple lesson. Every year the cost of production in human life is growing larger (50,000 killed, 100,000
wounded in America last year); the returns to the masses, who
help to create wealth, are ever getting smaller. Yet America
continues to be blind to the inevitable bankruptcy of our
business of production. Nor is this the only crime of the latter.
Still more fatal is the crime of turning the producer into a mere
particle of a machine, with less will and decision than his
master of steel and iron. Man is being robbed not merely of the
products of his labor, but of the power of free initiative, of
originality, and the interest in, or desire for, the things he is
making.

Real wealth consists in things of utility and beauty, in things
that help to create strong, beautiful bodies and surroundings
inspiring to live in. But if man is doomed to wind cotton
around a spool, or dig coal, or build roads for thirty years of
his life, there can be no talk of wealth. What he gives to the
world are only gray and hideous things, reflecting a dull and
hideous existence—too weak to live, too cowardly to die.
Strange to say, there are people who extol this deadening
method of centralized production as the proudest achievement
of our age. They fail utterly to realize that if we are to
continue in machine subserviency, our slavery is more complete than was our bondage to the King. They do not want to
know that centralization is not only the deathknell of liberty,
but also of health and beauty, of art and science, all these
being impossible in a clocklike, mechanical atmosphere.

Anarchism cannot but repudiate such a method of production: its goal is the freest possible expression of all the latent
powers of the individual. Oscar Wilde defines a perfect personality as "one who develops under perfect conditions, who is not
wounded, maimed, or in danger." A perfect personality, then,
is only possible in a state of society where man is free
to choose the mode of work, the conditions of work, and
the freedom to work. One to whom the making of a table,
the building of a house, or the tilling of the soil, is what the
painting is to the artist and the discovery to the scientist—the

result of inspiration, of intense longing, and deep interest in work as a creative force. That being the ideal of Anarchism, its economic arrangements must consist of voluntary productive and distributive associations, gradually developing into free communism, as the best means of producing with the least waste of human energy. Anarchism, however, also recognizes the right of the individual, or numbers of individuals, to arrange at all times for other forms of work, in harmony with their tastes and desires.

Such free display of human energy being possible only under complete individual and social freedom, Anarchism directs its forces against the third and greatest foe of all social equality; namely, the State, organized authority, or statutory law—the dominion of human conduct.

Just as religion has fettered the human mind, and as property, or the monopoly of things, has subdued and stifled man's needs, so has the State enslaved his spirit, dictating every phase of conduct. "All government in essence," says Emerson, "is tyranny." It matters not whether it is government by divine right or majority rule. In every instance its aim is the absolute subordination of the individual.

Referring to the American government, the greatest American Anarchist, David Thoreau, said: "Government, what is it but a tradition, though a recent one, endeavoring to transmit itself unimpaired to posterity, but each instance losing its integrity; it has not the vitality and force of a single living man. Law never made man a whit more just; and by means of their respect for it, even the well disposed are daily made agents of injustice."

Indeed, the keynote of government is injustice. With the arrogance and self-sufficiency of the King who could do no wrong, governments ordain, judge, condemn, and punish the most insignificant offenses, while maintaining themselves by the greatest of all offenses, the annihilation of individual liberty. Thus Ouida is right when she maintains that "the State only aims at instilling those qualities in its public by which its demands are obeyed, and its exchequer is filled. Its highest attainment is the reduction of mankind to clockwork. In its atmosphere all those finer and more delicate liberties, which require treatment and spacious expansion, inevitably dry up and perish. The State requires a taxpaying machine in which there is no hitch, an exchequer in which there is never a deficit, and a public, monotonous, obedient, colorless, spiritless, moving humbly like a flock of sheep along a straight high road between two walls."

Yet even a flock of sheep would resist the chicanery of the State, if it were not for the corruptive, tyrannical, and oppressive methods it employs to serve its purposes. Therefore Bakunin repudiates the State as synonymous with the surrender of the liberty of the individual or small minorities—the destruction of social relationship, the curtailment, or complete denial even, of life itself, for its own aggrandizement. The State is the altar of political freedom and, like the religious altar, it is maintained for the purpose of human sacrifice.

In fact, there is hardly a modern thinker who does not agree that government, organized authority, or the State, is necessary *only* to maintain or protect property and monopoly. It has proven efficient in that function only.

Even George Bernard Shaw, who hopes for the miraculous from the State under Fabianism, nevertheless admits that "it is at present a huge machine for robbing and slave-driving of the poor by brute force." This being the case, it is hard to see why the clever prefacer wishes to uphold the State after poverty shall have ceased to exist.

Unfortunately there are still a number of people who continue in the fatal belief that government rests on natural laws, that it maintains social order and harmony, that it diminishes crime, and that it prevents the lazy man from fleecing his fellows. I shall therefore examine these contentions.

A natural law is that factor in man which asserts itself freely and spontaneously without any external force, in harmony with the requirements of nature. For instance, the demand for nutrition, for sex gratification, for light, air, and exercise, is a natural law. But its expression needs not the machinery of government, needs not the club, the gun, the handcuff, or the prison. To obey such laws, if we may call it obedience, requires only spontaneity and free opportunity. That governments do not maintain themselves through such harmonious factors is proven by the terrible array of violence, force, and coercion all governments use in order to live. Thus Blackstone is right when he says, "Human laws are invalid, because they are contrary to the laws of nature."

Unless it be the order of Warsaw after the slaughter of thousands of people, it is difficult to ascribe to governments any capacity for order or social harmony. Order derived through submission and maintained by terror is not much of a safe guaranty; yet that is the only "order" that governments have ever maintained. True social harmony grows naturally out of solidarity of interests. In a society where those who always work never have anything, while those who never work enjoy everything, solidarity of interests is nonexistent; hence social harmony is but a myth. The only way organized authority meets this grave situation is by extending still greater privileges to those who have already monopolized the earth, and by still further enslaving the disinherited masses. Thus the entire arsenal of government—laws, police, soldiers, the courts, legislatures, prisons—is strenuously engaged in "harmonizing" the most antagonistic elements in society.

The most absurd apology for authority and law is that they serve to diminish crime. Aside from the fact that the State is itself the greatest criminal, breaking every written and natural law, stealing in the form of taxes, killing in the form of war and capital punishment, it has come to an absolute standstill in coping with crime. It has failed utterly to destroy or even minimize the horrible scourge of its own creation.

Crime is naught but misdirected energy. So long as every institution of today, economic, political, social, and moral, conspires to misdirect human energy into wrong channels; so long as most people are out of place doing the things they hate to do, living a life they loathe to live, crime will be inevitable, and all the laws on the statutes can only increase, but never do away with, crime. What does society, as it exists today, know of the process of despair, the poverty, the horrors, the fearful struggle the human soul must pass on its way to crime and degradation. Who that knows this terrible process can fail to see the truth in these words of Peter Kropotkin:

"Those who will hold the balance between the benefits thus attributed to law and punishment and the degrading effect of the latter on humanity; those who will estimate the torrent of depravity poured abroad in human society by the informer, favored by the Judge even, and paid for in clinking cash by governments, under the pretext of aiding to unmask crime; those who will go within prison walls and there see what human beings become when deprived of liberty, when subjected to the care of brutal keepers, to coarse, cruel words, to a thousand stinging, piercing humiliations, will agree with us that the entire apparatus of prison and punishment is an abomination which ought to brought to an end."

The deterrent influence of law on the lazy man is too absurd to merit consideration. If society were only relieved of the waste and expense of keeping a lazy class, and the equally great expense of the paraphernalia of protection this lazy class requires, the social tables would contain an abundance for all, including even the occasional lazy individual. Besides, it is well to consider that laziness results either from special privileges, or physical and mental abnormalities. Our present insane system of production fosters both, and the most astounding phenomenon is that people should want to work at all now. Anarchism aims to strip labor of its deadening, dulling aspect, of its gloom and compulsion. It aims to make work an instrument of joy, of strength, of color, of real harmony, so that the poorest sort of a man should find in work both recreation and hope.

To achieve such an arrangement of life, government, with its unjust, arbitrary, repressive measures, must be done away with. At best it has but imposed one single mode of life upon all, without regard to individual and social variations and needs. In destroying government and statutory laws, Anarchism proposes to rescue the self-respect and independence of the individual from all restraint and invasion by authority. Only in freedom can man grow to his full stature. Only in freedom will he learn to think and move, and give the very best in him. Only in freedom will he realize the true force of the social bonds which knit men together, and which are the true foundation of a normal social life.

But what about human nature? Can it be changed? And if not, will it endure under Anarchism?

Poor human nature, what horrible crimes have been committed in thy name! Every fool, from king to policeman, from the flatheaded parson to the visionless dabbler in science, presumes to speak authoritatively of human nature. The greater the mental charlatan, the more definite his insistence on the wickedness and weaknesses of human nature. Yet, how can any one speak of it today, with every soul in a prison, with every heart fettered, wounded, and maimed?

John Burroughs has stated that experimental study of animals in captivity is absolutely useless. Their character, their habits, their appetites undergo a complete transformation when torn from their soil in field and forest. With human nature caged in a narrow space, whipped daily into submission, how can we speak of its potentialities?

Freedom, expansion, opportunity, and, above all, peace and repose, alone can teach us the real dominant factors of human nature and all its wonderful possibilities.

Anarchism, then, really stands for the liberation of the human mind from the dominion of religion; the liberation of the human body from the dominion of property; liberation from the shackles and restraint of government. Anarchism stands for a social order based on the free grouping of individuals for the purpose of producing real social wealth; an order that will guarantee to every human being free access to the earth and full enjoyment of the necessities of life, according to individual desires, tastes, and inclinations.

This is not a wild fancy or an aberration of the mind. It is the conclusion arrived at by hosts of intellectual men and women the world over; a conclusion resulting from the close and studious observation of the tendencies of modern society: individual liberty and economic equality, the twin forces for the birth of what is fine and true in man.

As to methods. Anarchism is not, as some may suppose, a theory of the future to be realized through divine inspiration. It is a living force in the affairs of our life, constantly creating new conditions. The methods of Anarchism therefore do not comprise an iron-clad program to be carried out under all circumstances. Methods must grow out of the economic needs of each place and clime, and of the intellectual and temperamental requirements of the individual. The serene, calm character of a Tolstoy will wish different methods for social reconstruction than the intense, overflowing personality of a Michael Bakunin or a Peter Kropotkin. Equally so it must be apparent that the economic and political needs of Russia will dictate more drastic measures than would England or America. Anarchism does not stand for military drill and uniformity; it does, however, stand for the spirit of revolt, in whatever form, against everything that hinders human growth. All Anarchists agree in that, as they also agree in their opposition to the political machinery as a means of bringing about the great social change.

"All voting," says Thoreau, "is a sort of gaming, like checkers, or backgammon, a playing with right and wrong; its obligation never exceeds that of expediency. Even voting for the right thing is doing nothing for it. A wise man will not leave the right to the mercy of chance, nor wish it to prevail through the power of the majority." A close examination of the machinery of politics and its achievements will bear out the logic of Thoreau.

What does the history of parliamentarism show? Nothing but failure and defeat, not even a single reform to ameliorate the economic and social stress of the people. Laws have been passed and enactments made for the improvement and protection of labor. Thus it was proven only last year that Illinois, with the most rigid laws for mine protection, had the greatest mine disasters. In States where child labor laws prevail, child exploitation is at its highest, and though with us the workers enjoy full political opportunities, capitalism has reached the most brazen zenith.

Even were the workers able to have their own representatives, for which our good Socialist politicians are clamoring, what chances are there for their honesty and good faith? One has but to bear in mind the process of politics to realize that its path of good intentions is full of pitfalls: wirepulling, intriguing, flattering, lying, cheating; in fact, chicanery of every description, whereby the political aspirant can achieve success. Added to that is a complete demoralization of character and conviction, until nothing is left that would make one hope for anything from such a human derelict. Time and time again the people were foolish enough to trust, believe, and support with their last farthing aspiring politicians, only to find themselves betrayed and cheated.

It may be claimed that men of integrity would not become corrupt in the political grinding mill. Perhaps not; but such men would be absolutely helpless to exert the slightest influence in behalf of labor, as indeed has been shown in numerous instances. The State is the economic master of its servants. Good men, if such there be, would either remain true to their political faith and lose their economic support, or they would cling to their economic master and be utterly unable to do the slightest good. The political arena leaves one no alternative, one must either be a dunce or a rogue.

The political superstition is still holding sway over the hearts and minds of the masses, but the true lovers of liberty will have no more to do with it. Instead, they believe with Stirner that man has as much liberty as he is willing to take. Anarchism therefore stands for direct action, the open defiance of, and resistance to, all laws and restrictions, economic, social, and moral. But defiance and resistance are illegal. Therein lies the salvation of man. Everything illegal necessitates integrity, self-reliance, and courage. In short, it calls for free, independent spirits, for "men who are men, and who have a bone in their backs which you cannot pass your hand through."

Universal suffrage itself owes its existence to direct action. If not for the spirit of rebellion, of the defiance on the part of the American revolutionary fathers, their posterity would still wear the King's coat. If not for the direct action of a John Brown and his comrades, America would still trade in the flesh of the black man. True, the trade in white flesh is still going on; but that, too, will have to be abolished by direct action. Trade-unionism, the economic arena of the modern gladiator, owes its existence to direct action. It is but recently that law and government have attempted to crush the trade-union movement, and condemned the exponents of man's right to organize to prison as conspirators. Had they sought to assert their cause through begging, pleading, and compromise, trade-unionism would today be a negligible quantity. In France, in Spain, in Italy, in Russia, nay even in England (witness the growing rebellion of English labor unions), direct, revolutionary, economic action has become so strong a force in the battle for industrial liberty as to make the world realize the tremendous importance of labor's power. The General Strike, the supreme expression of the economic consciousness of the workers, was ridiculed in America but a short time ago. Today every great strike, in order to win, must realize the importance of the solidaric general protest.

Direct action, having proven effective along economic lines, is equally potent in the environment of the individual. There a hundred forces encroach upon his being, and only persistent resistance to them will finally set him free. Direct action against the authority in the shop, direct action against the authority of the law, direct action against the invasive, meddlesome authority of our moral code, is the logical, consistent method of Anarchism.

Will it not lead to a revolution? Indeed, it will. No real social change has ever come about without a revolution. People are either not familiar with their history, or they have not yet learned that revolution is but thought carried into action.

Anarchism, the great leaven of thought, is today permeating every phase of human endeavor. Science, art, literature, the drama, the effort for economic betterment, in fact every individual and social opposition to the existing disorder of things, is illumined by the spiritual light of Anarchism. It is the philosophy of the sovereignty of the individual. It is the theory of social harmony. It is the great, surging, living truth that is reconstructing the world, and that will usher in the Dawn.

5 An Anarchist's View of Democracy

PIERRE-JOSEPH PROUDHON

This pamphlet was written a few weeks after the February 1848 Revolution in Paris had replaced the constitutional monarchy of King Louis-Philippe with a nominally democratic republic. Proudhon insisted that people should rule themselves, but maintained that democratic government cannot in fact make this possible, despite its claims to do so. Here he gives in relatively brief form some of the arguments he develops much further in later writings. While in this piece he discusses the politics of France in 1848, his criticisms have much wider import.

Heaven, listen; Earth, lend an ear: the Lord has spoken!

Thus cried the prophets when, their eyes gleaming and mouths foaming, they proclaimed punishment to liars and apostates for their sins. Thus spoke the Church in the middle ages, and mankind, prostrate with fear, crossed itself at the voice of the pontiff and the injunctions of his bishops. Thus it was by turns with Moses, Elijah, John the Baptist, Mohammed, Luther, all the founders and reformers of religions, each new modification of dogma claiming to emanate from divine authority. And always the masses of humanity were seen prostrating themselves at the name of the Most High, and

Excerpts from "Solution du problème social," *Oeuvres complètes de P.-J. Proudhon* (Paris: A. Lacroix, Verboeckhoven et Cie., 1867–70), VI, 1–87. Translation, pp. 35–40, 42–44, 46–58, 60, 62–67, by the editor and S. Valerie Hoffman.

receiving submissively the discipline of the bearers of revelation.

But finally a philosopher said to himself, if God has spoken, why have I heard nothing?

This word of doubt sufficed to shake the Church, nullify the Scriptures, dissipate the faith, and hasten the reign of the Antichrist!

Like Hume, I do not want at all to prejudge either the reality or the possibility of a revelation: how can one reason *a priori* about a supernatural event, a manifestation of the Supreme Being? For me the issue is entirely one of the empirical knowledge of it that we can attain, and I reduce the religious controversy to this single point, the authenticity of the divine word. Prove this authenticity, and I am a Christian. Who then would dare dispute with God, if he were sure that it is God who speaks to him?

It is the same with the People as with the Divinity: *Vox populi, vox Dei.*

Since the beginning of the world, since human tribes began to organize themselves into monarchies and republics, oscillating between the one idea and the other like wandering planets, mixing, combining in order to organize the most diverse elements into societies, overturning tribunes and thrones as a child upsets a house of cards, we have seen, at each political upheaval, the leaders of the movement invoke in more or less explicit terms the sovereignty of the People. . . .

The most prominent spokesman of the Bourbon monarchists would tell us still, if it dared, that law results from the consent of the People and the enunciation of the prince: *Lex fit consensu populi et constitutione regis.* The sovereignty of the nation is the first principle of monarchists as of democrats. Listen to the echo which reaches us from the North: on the one hand, there is a despotic king who invokes national traditions—that is, the will of the People expressed and confirmed over the centuries. On the other, there are subjects in revolt who maintain that the People no longer think what they did formerly, and who ask that the People be consulted. Who then

52   *An Anarchist's View of Democracy*

shows here a better understanding of the People—the monarch who would have it that they are unchangeable in their thinking, or the citizens who suppose them changeable? And when you say the contradiction is resolved by progress, meaning that the People go through different phases before arriving at the same old idea, you only increase the difficulty: who will judge what is progress and what is retrogression?

I ask then, like Rousseau: If the People has spoken, why have I heard nothing?

You point out to me this astonishing revolution in which I too have taken part—whose legitimacy I myself have proven, whose idea I have brought to the fore. And you say to me: There is the People!

But in the first place, I have seen only a tumultuous crowd without awareness of the ideas that made it act, without any comprehension of the revolution brought about by its hands. Then what I have called the logic of the People could well be nothing but recognition of past events, all the more so since once it is all over and everyone agrees on their significance, opinions are divided anew as to the consequences. The revolution over, the People says nothing! What then! Does the sovereignty of the People exist only for things in the past, which no longer interest us, and not at all for those of the future, which alone can be the objects of the People's decrees?

Oh all you enemies of despotism and its corruption, as of anarchy and its piracy, who never cease invoking the People— you who speak frankly of its sovereign reason, its irresistible strength, its formidable voice, I bid you tell me: Where and when have you heard the People? With what mouths, in what language do they express themselves? How is this astonishing revelation accomplished? What authentic, conclusive examples do you cite? What guarantee have you of the validity of these laws you say issue from the People? What is the sanction? By what claims, by what signs, shall I distinguish the elect delegated by the People from the apostates who take advantage of its trust and usurp its authority? When you come right down to it, how do you establish the legitimacy of the popular Word?

I believe in the existence of the People as I do in the existence of God.

I bow before its holy will; I submit to all orders coming hence; the People's word is my law, my strength, and my hope. But, following the precept of Saint Paul, to be worthy my obedience must be rational, and what a misfortune for me, what ignominy, if, while believing myself to be submitting only to the People's authority, I were to be the plaything of a vile charlatan! How then, I beg of you, among so many rival apostles, contradictory opinions, and obstinate partisans, am I to recognize the voice, the true voice of the People?

The problem of the sovereignty of the People is the funda-mental problem of liberty, equality, and fraternity, the first principle of social organization. Governments and peoples have had no other goal, through all the storms of revolutions and diversions of politics, than to constitute this sovereignty. Each time that they have been diverted from this goal they have fallen into slavery and shame. With this in mind the Provision-al Government has convened a National Assembly named by all citizens, without distinction as to wealth and capacity: universal suffrage seems to them to be the closest approach to expressing the People's sovereignty.

Thus it is supposed first that the People can be consulted; second, that it can respond; third, that its will can be authenti-cally ascertained; and finally that government founded upon the manifest will of the People is the only legitimate govern-ment.

In particular, such is the pretension of DEMOCRACY, which presents itself as the form of government which best translates the sovereignty of the People.

But, if I prove that democracy, just like monarchy, only symbolizes that sovereignty, that it does not respond to any of the questions raised by this idea, that it can not, for example, either establish the authenticity of the actions attributed to the People or state what is the final goal of society; if I prove that democracy, far from being the most perfect of governments, is the negation of the sovereignty of the People and the origin of its ruin—it will be demonstrated, in fact and in right, that democracy is nothing more than a constitutional despotism, succeeding a different constitutional despotism, that it does not possess any scientific value, and that it must be seen solely as a preparation for the REPUBLIC, one and indivisible.

It is important to clarify opinion on this point immediately, and to eliminate all illusion.

The People, the collective being—I almost said rational being—does not speak at all in the true sense of the word. The People, no more than God, has no eyes to see, no ears to hear, no mouth to speak. How do I know if it is endowed with some sort of soul, a divinity immanent in the masses, as certain philosophers hypothesize a world soul, and which at certain moments moves and urges it on; or whether the reason of the People is none other than pure idea, the most abstract, the most comprehensive, the freest of all individual form, as other philosophers claim that God is simply the order in the universe, an abstraction? I am not getting involved in the investigations of esoteric psychology: as a practical man I ask in what manner this soul, reason, will, or what have you is set outside itself, so to speak, and makes itself known? Who can serve as its spokesman? Who has the right to say to others, "It is through me that the People speaks"? How shall I believe that he who harangues five hundred applauding individuals from atop a soapbox is the People's spokesman? How does the election by citizens, nay even their unanimous vote, have the faculty of conferring this sort of privilege, to serve as the People's interpreter? And when you show me, like a coterie, nine hundred personages thus chosen by their fellow citizens, why ought I believe that these nine hundred delegates, who do not all agree among each other, are prompted by a mysterious inspiration from the People? And, when all is said, how will the law they are going to make obligate me?

Here is a president or a directory, the personification, symbol, or fabrication of national sovereignty: the first power of the State.

Here are a chamber, two chambers—one the spokesman of conservative interests, the other of the instinct for development: the second power of the State.

Here is a press, eloquent, disciplined, untiring, which each morning pours out in torrents millions of ideas which swarm in the millions of brains of the citizenry: the third power of the State.

The executive power is action, the chambers—deliberation, the press—opinion.

Which of these powers represents the people? Or else, if you say that it is the whole thing which represents the people, how is it that they do not all agree? Put royalty in place of the presidency, and it is the same thing: my criticisms apply equally to monarchy and democracy. . . .

And what do we hear from the platform? And what does the Government know? Not so long ago it was escaping its responsibilities by denying its own authority to make decisions. It did not exist, it claimed, in order to organize work and give bread to the People. For a month it has received the demands of the proletariat; for a month it has been at work—and for a month it has had the official gazette publish every day this great news: that it knows nothing, that it discovers nothing! The Government divides the People; it arouses hatred between the classes that compose it. But to organize the People, to create that sovereignty which is simultaneously liberty and accord, this exceeds the Government's ability, as formerly it exceeded its jurisdiction. In a Government which calls itself instituted by the People's will such remarkable ignorance is a contradiction: it is apparent that already the People is sovereign no longer.

Does the People, which is sometimes said to have risen like a single man, also think like one man? Reflect? Reason? Make conclusions? Does it have a memory, imagination, ideas? If in reality the People is sovereign, it thinks; if it thinks, doubtless it has its own way of thinking and formulating its thought. How then does the People think? What are the forms of popular reasoning? Does it proceed by means of categories? Does it employ syllogism, induction, analysis, antinomy, or analogy? Is

it Aristotelian or Hegelian? You must explain all that; otherwise, your respect for the sovereignty of the People is only
absurd fetishism. One might as well worship a stone.

Does the People call upon experience in its meditations?
Does it bear in mind its memories, or else is its course to
produce new ideas endlessly? How does it reconcile respect for
its traditions with its needs for development? How does it finish
with one worn-out hypothesis and go on to try another? What
is the law of its transitions and its movement from one idea to
the next? What stimulates it, what defines the course of its
progress? Why this moving about, this instability? I need to
know all this—otherwise the law you impose on me in the
name of the People ceases to be authentic: it is no longer law,
but violence.

Does the People always think? And if it does not, how do
you account for the intermittent character of its thought? If we
suppose that the People can be represented, what will its
representatives do during these interruptions? Does the People
sleep sometimes, like Jupiter in the arms of Juno? When does
it dream? When does it stay awake? You must teach me about
all these things; otherwise, the power you exercise by delegation from the People being only interim, and the length of the
interim being unknown, this power is usurped: you are inclined
toward tyranny.

If the People thinks, reflects, reasons, sometimes *a priori,*
according to the rules of pure reason, sometimes *a posteriori*
upon the data of experience, it runs the risk of deceiving itself.
Then it no longer suffices, for me to accept the People's
thought as law, that its authenticity be proven to me; it is
necessary that the thought itself be legitimate. Who will choose
among the ideas and fantasies of the People? To whom shall
we appeal its will, which may be erroneous, and consequently
despotic?

Here I present this dilemma:

If the People can err, then there are two alternatives. On the
one hand, the error may seem as respectable as if it were true,
and can claim complete obedience despite the error. In this

case the People is a supremely immoral being, since it can simultaneously think, will, and do evil.

On the other hand, ought we find fault with the People in its errors? There would then be, in certain cases, a duty for a government to resist the People! Who will tell it: You deceive yourself! Who will be able to set it to rights, to restrain it?

But what am I saying? If the People is liable to err, what becomes of its sovereignty? Is it not evident that the People's will should be taken into consideration all the less as it is more formidable in its consequences, and that the true principle of all politics, the guarantee of the security of nations, is to consult the People only in order to distrust it? Can not all inspiration from it hide immense peril as much as immense success, and its will be only a suicidal thought?

Doubtless, you will say, the People has only a mystical existence. It manifests itself only at rare intervals, in predestined epochs! But for all that the People is no phantom, and when it rises, no one can fail to recognize it. . . .

Now if the People has, in all historical epochs, thought, expressed, willed, and done a multitude of contradictory things; if, even today, among so many opinions which divide it, it is impossible for it to choose one without repudiating another and consequently without being self-contradictory—what do you want me to think of the reason, the morality, the justice, of its acts? What can I expect of its representatives? And what proof of authenticity will you give me in favor of an opinion, such that I can not immediately make a claim for the contrary one?

What astonishes me in the midst of the confusion of ideas, is that faith in the sovereignty of the People, far from dwindling, seems by this very confusion to reach its own climax. In this obstinant belief of the multitude in the intelligence which exists within it I see a sort of manifestation of the People which affirms itself, like Jehovah, and says, "I AM." I can not then deny, on the contrary, I am forced to confess the sovereignty of the People. But beyond this initial affirmation, and when it is a question of going from the subject of the thought to its object, when in other words it is a question of applying the criterion to acts of Government, let someone tell me, where is the People?

In principle then, I admit that the People exists, that it is sovereign, that it is predicated in the consciousness of the masses. But nothing yet has proven to me that it can perform an overt act of sovereignty, that an explicit revelation of the People is possible. For, in view of the dominance of prejudices, of the contradiction of ideas and interests, of the variability of opinion, and of the impulsiveness of the multitude, I shall always ask what establishes the authenticity and legitimacy of such a revelation—and this is what democracy can not answer.

But, the democrats observe—not without reason—the People has never been suitably called to action. Never has it been able to demonstrate its will except for momentary flashes: the role it has played in history up to now has been completely subordinate. For the People to be able to speak its mind, it must be democratically consulted—that is, all citizens without distinction must participate, directly or indirectly, in the formation of the law. Now, this mode of democratic consultation has never been exercised in a coherent manner: the eternal conspiracy of the privileged has not permitted it. Princes, nobles and priests, military men, magistrates, teachers, scholars, artists, industrialists, merchants, financiers, proprietors, have always succeeded in breaking up the democratic union, in changing the voice of the People into a voice of monopoly. Now that we possess the only true way of having the People speak, we shall likewise know what constitutes the authenticity and legitimacy of its word, and all your preceding objections vanish. The sincerity of the democratic regime will guarantee the solution to us. . . .

According to the theory of universal suffrage, experience should have proven that the middle class, which alone has exercised political rights of late, does not represent the People— far from it, with the monarchy it has been in constant reaction against the People.

One concludes that it is up to the entire nation to name its representatives.

But won't it be only an artificial representation, just the product of the arbitrary will of the electoral mob, if the representatives come from one class of men who provide the free, upward flight of society, the spontaneous development of sciences, arts, industry, and commerce, the necessity of institutions, the tacit consent or the well-known incapacity of the lower classes, one class finally whose talent and wealth designates them as the *natural* elite of the People? Won't it be thus with representatives chosen by electoral meetings of varying completeness, enlightenment, and freedom, and which act under the influence of local passions, prejudices, and hatred for persons and principles?

We shall have an aristocracy of our own choice—I have no objection—in place of a natural aristocracy; but aristocracy for aristocracy I prefer, with M. Guizot, that of fatality to that of arbitrary will: fatality puts me under no obligation.

Or, rather, we will only restore, by another route, the same aristocrats; for whom do you want named to represent them, these working stiffs, these day laborers, these toilers, if not their bourgeoisie? Unless you only want that they kill them!

One way or another, preponderant strength in government belongs to the men who have the preponderance of talent and fortune. From the first it has been evident that social reform will never come out of political reform, that on the contrary political reform must come out of social reform.

The illusion of democracy springs from that of constitutional monarchy's example—claiming to organize Government by representative means. Neither the Revolution of July [1830], nor that of February [1848] has sufficed to illuminate this. What they always want is inequality of fortunes, delegation of sovereignty, and government by influential people. Instead of saying, as did M. Thiers, *The king reigns and does not govern,* democracy says, *The People reigns and does not govern,* which is to deny the Revolution. . . .

Since, according to the ideology of the democrats, the People can not govern itself and is forced to give itself to representatives who govern by delegation, while it retains the right of review, it is supposed that the People is quite capable at least of having itself represented, that it can be represented faithfully. Well! This hypothesis is utterly false; there is not and never can be legitimate representation of the People. All electoral systems are mechanisms for deceit: to know one is sufficient to pronounce the condemnation of all.

Take the example of the Provisional Government [just established]. . . .

Its system pretends to be universal, but whatever it does, in the entire electoral system there will always be exclusions, absences, and votes which are invalidated, erroneous, or unfree. The hardiest innovators have not yet dared to demand suffrage for women, children, domestic servants, or men with criminal records. About four-fifths of the People are not represented, and are cut off from the communion of the People. Why?

You fix electoral capacity at twenty-one years' age; why not twenty? Why not at nineteen, eighteen, seventeen? What! One year, one day makes the elector rational! A Barra or Viala is incapable of voting discerningly while the Fouchés and Héberts vote for them!

You eliminate women. You have thus resolved the grand problem of the inferiority of the sex. What! No exception for Lucretia, Cornelia, Joan of Arc or Charlotte Corday! A Roland, a Staël, a George Sand will find no favor before your manhood! The Jacobins welcomed the revolutionary women who sat knitting at their meetings; no one has ever said that the presence of these citizenesses weakened the courage of the citizens!

You set aside the domestic servant. You are saying that this sign of servitude does not cover a generous soul, that in the heart of a valet beats no idea which will save the Republic! Is the race of Figaro lost? It is the fault of this man, you will say:

why, with so many abilities, is he a servant? And why are there servants?

I want to see, I want to hear the People in its variety and multitude, all ages, all sexes, all conditions, all virtues, all miseries: for all that, this is the People.

You claim that there would be grievous trouble for good discipline, for the peace of the State and tranquillity of families, if women, children, and domestic servants obtained the same rights as husbands, fathers, and masters, that in addition the former are adequately represented by the latter through their solidarity of interests and the familial bond.

I acknowledge that the objection is a serious one, and I do not attempt to refute it. But take care: you must, by the same reasoning, exclude the proletarians and all workers. Seven-tenths of this category receive the aid of public charity: they will then go on to vote themselves government jobs, salary increases, labor reductions, and they will not fail in this, I assure you, if their delegates represent them ever so little. In the National Assembly the proletariat will be like the officials in M. Guizot's Chamber, judging its own cause, having power over the budget and putting nothing there, creating dictatorship by their appointments, until, with capital exhausted by taxation and property producing nothing any longer, general bankruptcy breaks apart this parliamentary beggary.

And all these citizens who, because of work, sickness, travel, or lack of money to go to the elections, are forced to abstain from voting, how do you count them? Will it be according to the proverb, "Who says nothing, consents"? But, consents to what? To the opinion of the majority, or indeed to that of the minority?

And those who vote only on impulse, through good-nature or interest, through faith in their republican committee or parish priest: what do you make of them? It is an old maxim that in all deliberations it is necessary not only to count the votes, but to weigh them. In your committees, on the contrary, the vote of an Arago or Lamartine counts no more than that of a beggar.

Will you say that the consideration due men for their merit is secured by the influence they exercise on the electors? Then the voting is not free. It is the voices of ability that we hear, not that of the People. One might as well preserve electoral suffrage based on qualification by ownership of property. . . .

I pass over in silence the material and moral impossibilities which abound in the mode of election adopted by the Provisional Government. It is completely devoted to the opinion that in doubling the national representation and making people vote for inseparable lists of candidates, the Provisional Government wanted the citizens to choose not men but principle, precisely in the manner of the former Government, which also made people vote on the system, not on the men. How is one to discuss the choice of ten, twenty, twenty-five deputies? How, if each citizen votes freely and in knowledge of his cause, are the votes of such elections-by-list to be counted? How are such elections brought to a conclusion, if they are serious? Evidently it is impossible.

I do not discuss, I repeat, the purely material side of the question: I keep to issues of right. What formerly was obtained through venality, today they extort from impotence. They say to the elector: Here are our friends, the friends of the Republic; and there are our adversaries, who also are the adversaries of the Republic—choose. And the elector who can not appraise the abilities of the candidates votes out of confidence!

Instead of naming deputies for each district, as under the fallen regime, they will have them elected by province. They wanted, by this measure, to destroy the spirit of localism. How wonderful it is that the democrats are so sure of their principles!

If the deputies, they say, are named by districts, it is not France which is represented, but the districts. The national Assembly would no longer be representative of the country; it would be a congress of 459 separate delegations.

Why then, I reply, don't you have each elector name the deputies for all France?

It would be desirable, you answer, but it is impossible.

I observe first that any system which can be true only in conditions themselves impossible seems to me a poor system. But to me the democrats here appear singularly inconsistent and perplexed by mere trifles. If the representatives ought to represent not the provinces, nor the districts, nor the towns, nor the countryside, nor industry, nor commerce, nor agriculture, nor special interests, but only FRANCE!—then why have they decided that there should be one deputy per 40,000 inhabitants? Why not one per 100,000 or 200,000! Ninety instead of nine hundred—wouldn't that suffice? Couldn't you in Paris, cut short your list of candidates, while the conservatives and the various royalists cut short theirs? Was it more difficult to vote on a list of ninety names than on one of fifteen?

But who does not see that deputies thus elected apart from all special interests and groups, all considerations of places and persons, by dint of representing France, represent nothing; that they no longer are mandated representatives, but legislators set apart from the People; and that in place of a representative democracy we have an elective oligarchy, the middle term between democracy and royalty.

There, citizen reader, is where I want to bring you. From whatever aspect you consider democracy, you will always see it placed between two extremes each as contrary as the other to its own principle, condemned to oscillate between the absurd and the impossible, without ever being able to establish itself. Among a million equally arbitrary terms, the Provisional Government has acted like M. Guizot: it has preferred that which appeared to it to agree best with its democratic prejudices. Of representative truth, as of government of the People by the People, the Provisional Government has taken no account. . . .

In order that the deputy represent his constituents, it is necessary that he represent all the ideas which have united to elect him.

But, with the electoral system, the deputy, the would-be legislator sent by the citizens to reconcile all ideas and all interests in the name of the People, always represents just one idea, one interest. The rest is excluded without pity. For who makes law in the elections? Who decides the choice of deputies? The majority, half plus one of the votes. From this it follows that half less one of the electors is not represented or is so in spite of itself, that of all the opinions that divide the citizens, one only, insofar as the deputy has an opinion, arrives at the legislature, and finally that the law, which should be the expression of the will of the People, is only the expression of half of the People.

The result is that in the theory of the democrats the problem consists of eliminating, by the mechanism of sham universal suffrage, all ideas save one which stir opinion, and to declare sovereign that which has the majority.

But, perhaps it will be said, the idea that fails in such an electoral body will triumph in another and, by this means, all ideas can be represented in the National Assembly.

When that is the case, you would have only put off the difficulty, for the question is to know how all these ideas, divergent and antagonistic, will concur on the law and be reconciled thereon.

Thus the Revolution, according to some, is only an accident, which should change nothing in the general order of society. According to others, the Revolution is social still more than political. How can such obviously incompatible claims be satisfied? How at the same time can there be given security for the bourgeoisie and guarantees for the proletariat? How will these contrary wishes and opposed inclinations come to be mixed together in a resulting community, in one universal law?

Democracy is so far from being able to resolve this difficulty that all its art, all its science is used to remove the obstacle. It makes appeals to the ballot box; the ballot box is simultaneously the level, the balance, the criterion of democracy. With the electoral ballot democracy eliminates men; with the legislative ballot, it eliminates ideas. . . .

What! It is one vote that makes the representative, one vote that makes the law! With a question on which hangs the honor and health of the Republic, the citizens are divided into two equal factions. On the two sides they bring to bear the most serious reasoning, the weightiest authorities, the most positive facts. The nation is in doubt, the Assembly is in suspension. One representative, without discernible motive, passes from right to left and turns the balance; it is he who makes the law.

And this law, the expression of some bizarre will, is supposed to be the will of the People! It will be necessary for me to submit to it, defend it, even kill for it! By a parliamentary caprice I lose the most precious of my rights, I lose liberty! And the most sacred of my duties, the duty to resist tyranny by force, falls before the sovereign noggin of an imbecile!

Democracy is nothing but the tyranny of majorities, the most execrable tyranny of all, for it is not based on the authority of a religion, nor on a nobility of blood, nor on the prerogatives of fortune: it has number as its base, and for a mask the name of the People. . . .

If universal suffrage, the most complete manifestation of democracy, has won so many partisans, especially among the working classes, it is because it has always been presented on the basis of an appeal to men of talent, as well as to the good sense and morality of the masses. How often have they not brought out the offensive contrast of the speculator who becomes politically influential through plunder and the man of genius whom poverty has kept far away from the stage! . . .

In the end, we are all electors; we can choose the most worthy.

We can do more; we can follow them step by step in their legislative acts and their votes; we shall make them transmit our arguments and our documents; we shall indicate our will to them, and when we are discontented, we shall recall and dismiss them.

The choice of abilities, imperative mandate, permanent revocability—these are the most immediate and incontestable consequences of the electoral principle. It is the inevitable program of all democracy.

Now democracy, no more than constitutional monarchy, does not sustain such a deduction from its principle.

What democracy demands, like monarchy, is silent deputies

who do not discuss, but vote; who, receiving the order from the Government, crush the opposition with their heavy and heavy-witted battalions. These are passive creatures, I almost say satellites, whom the danger of a revolution does not intimidate, whose reason is not too rebellious, whose conscience does not recoil before anything arbitrary, before any proscription. . . .

. . . In every kind of government the deputy belongs to the powerful, not to the country. . . . [It is required] that he be master of his vote, that is, to traffic in its sale, that the mandate have a specified term, of at least a year, during which the Government, in agreement with the deputies, does what it pleases and gives strength to the law through action by its own arbitrary will. . . .

If monarchy is the hammer which crushes the People, democracy is the axe which divides it: the one and the other equally conclude in the death of liberty. . . .

[Because theorists] have taught that all power has its source in national sovereignty, it has valiantly been concluded best to make all citizens vote in one way or another, and that the majority of votes thus expressed adequately constitute the will of the People. They have brought us back to the practices of barbarians who, lacking rationality, proceeded by acclamation and election. They have taken a material symbol for the true formula of sovereignty. And they have said to the proletarians: When you vote, you shall be free, you shall be rich; you shall enact capital, product and wages; you shall, as another Moses did, make thrushes and manna fall from heaven; you shall become like gods, for you shall not work, or shall work so little that if you do work it shall be as nothing.

Whatever they do and whatever they say, universal suffrage, the testimony of discord, can only produce discord. And it is with this miserable idea, I am ashamed for my native land, that for seventeen years they have agitated the poor People! It is for this that bourgeoisie and workers have sung the "Marseillaise" in chorus at seventy political banquets and, after a revolution as glorious as it was legitimate, have abandoned themselves to a sect of doctrinaires! For six months the opposition deputies, like comedians on tour, travelled through the provinces, and for the fruit of their benefit performance what have they brought back to us, what? A scheme for land redistribution! It is under this schismatic flag that we have claimed to preserve the initiative of progress, to march at the forefront of nations in the conquest of liberty, to inaugurate harmony around the world! Yesterday, we regarded with pity the peoples who did not know as we have how to raise themselves to constitutional sublimity. Today, fallen a hundred times lower, we still are sorry for them, we shall go with a hundred thousand bayonets to make them partake with us of the benefits of democratic absolutism. And we are the great nation! Oh! Be quiet, and if you do not know how to do great things, or express great ideas, at least preserve common sense for us. . . .

In monarchy, the acts of the Government are an unfolding of authority; in democracy they constitute authority. The authority which in monarchy is the principle of governmental action is the goal of government in democracy. The result is that democracy is fatally retrograde, and that it implies contradiction.

Let us place ourselves at the point of departure for democracy, at the moment of universal suffrage.

All citizens are equal, independent. Their egalitarian combination is the point of departure for power: it is power itself, in its highest form, in its plenitude.

By virtue of democratic principle, all citizens must participate in the formation of the law, in the government of the State, in the exercise of public functions, in the discussion of the budget, in the appointment of officials. All must be consulted and give their opinions on peace and war, treaties of commerce and alliance, colonial enterprises, works of public utility, the award of compensation, the infliction of penalties. Finally, all must pay their debt to their native land, as taxpayers, jurors, judges, and soldiers.

If things could happen in this way, the ideal of democracy would be attained. It would have a normal existence, developing directly in the sense of its principle, as do all things which have life and grow. It is thus that the acorn becomes an oak, and the embryo an animal; it is thus that geometry, astronomy, chemistry are the development to infinity of a small number of elements.

It is completely otherwise in democracy, which according to the authors exists fully only at the moment of elections and for the formation of legislative power. This moment once past, democracy retreats; it withdraws into itself again, and begins its anti-democratic work. It becomes AUTHORITY. Authority was the idol of M. Guizot; it is also that of the democrats.

In fact it is not true, in any democracy, that all citizens participate in the formation of the law: that prerogative is reserved for the representatives.

It is not true that they deliberate on all public affairs, domestic and foreign: this is the perquisite, not even of the representatives, but of the ministers. Citizens discuss affairs, ministers alone deliberate them.

It is not true that each citizen fulfills a public function: those functions which do not produce marketable goods must be reduced as much as possible. By their nature public functions exclude the vast majority of citizens. . . .

It is not true that citizens participate in the nomination of officials; moreover this participation is as impossible as the preceding one, since it would result in creating anarchy in the bad sense of the word. It is power which names its subordinates, sometimes according to its own arbitrary will, sometimes according to certain conditions for appointment or promotion, the order and discipline of officials and centralization requiring that it be thus. . . .

Finally, it is not true that all citizens participate in justice and in war: as judges and officers, most are eliminated; as jurors and simple soldiers all abstain as much as they can. In a word, hierarchy in government being the primary condition of government, democracy is a chimera.

The reason that authors give for this merits our study. They say the People is outside the state because it does not know how to govern itself, and when it does know, it can not do it.

EVERYBODY CAN NOT COMMAND AND GOVERN AT THE SAME TIME; it is necessary that the authority belong solely to some who exercise it in the name of and through the delegation of all.

Ignorance or impotence, according to democratic theory the People is incapable of governing itself: democracy, like monarchy, after having posed as its principle the sovereignty of the People, ends with a declaration of the *incapacity of the People!*

This is what is meant by the democrats, who once in the government dream only of consolidating and strengthening the authority in their hands. Thus it was understood by the multitude, who threw themselves upon the doors of the City Hall, demanding government jobs, money, work, credit, bread! And there indeed is our nation, monarchist to its very marrow, idolizing power, deprived of individual energy and republican initiative, accustomed to expect everything from authority, to do nothing except through authority! When monarchy does not come to us from on high, as it did formerly, or on the field of battle, as in 1800, or in the folds of a charter, as in 1814 or 1830, we proclaim it in the public square, between two barricades, in electoral assembly, or at a patriotic banquet. Drink to the health of the People and the multitude will crown you!

6 Patriotism and Government

LEO TOLSTOY

Leo Tolstoy (1828–1910), though more widely known as a great novelist, also was distinguished by an exceptional personal religious faith which caused him to commit himself to anarchism and Christian pacifism, writing extensively on his moral convictions. Few anarchists would accept Tolstoy's religious beliefs and absolute pacifism, but most would agree with what he says here. Although the premises and perspectives of pacifists and anarchists usually are quite different, they are often quite close in their conclusions; one major link is the thought of Tolstoy.

> The time is fast approaching when to call a man a patriot will be the deepest insult you can offer him. Patriotism now means advocating plunder in the interests of the privileged classes of the particular State system into which we have happened to be born.—E. BELFORT BAX.

I have already several times expressed the thought that in our day the feeling of patriotism is an unnatural, irrational, and harmful feeling, the cause of a great part of the ills from which mankind is suffering, and that consequently this feeling should not be cultivated, as it now is, but should on the contrary be suppressed and eradicated by all rational means. Yet strange to say—though it is undeniable that the universal armaments and destructive wars which are ruining the peoples result from that one feeling—all my arguments showing the backwardness, anachronism, and harmfulness of patriotism have been and still are met either by silence, by intentional misinterpretation, or by a strange unvarying reply to the effect

From *Kingdom of God and Peace Essays*, translated by Louise and Aylmer Maude (London: Oxford University Press, 1935), pp. 545–61, 569–574. The essay, written in 1900, is here somewhat condensed.

that only bad patriotism (Jingoism, or Chauvinism) is evil, but that real good patriotism is a very elevated moral feeling to condemn which is not only irrational but wicked.

What this real, good patriotism consists in, we are never told. If anything is said about it we get declamatory, inflated phrases, instead of explanation, or else some other conception is substituted—something which has nothing in common with the patriotism we all know and from the results of which we suffer so severely.

It is generally said that the real, good patriotism consists in desiring for one's own people or State such real benefits as do not infringe the well-being of other nations.

Talking recently to an Englishman about the present war [the Boer War] I said to him that the real cause of the war was not avarice, as was generally said, but patriotism, as the whole temper of English society showed. The Englishman did not agree with me, and said that even were it so it merely showed that the patriotism at present inspiring Englishmen is a bad patriotism; but that good patriotism, such as he was imbued with, would cause his English compatriots to act well.

"Then do you wish only Englishmen to act well?" I asked.

"I wish all men to do so," said he, indicating clearly by that reply the characteristic of true benefits whether moral, scientific, or even material and practical—which is that they spread out to all men. But to wish such benefits to everyone is evidently not only not patriotic but the reverse.

Neither do the peculiarities of each people constitute patriotism, though these things are purposely substituted for the conception of patriotism by its defenders. They say that the peculiarities of each people are an essential condition of human progress, and that patriotism, which seeks to maintain those peculiarities, is therefore a good and useful feeling. But is it not quite evident that if, once upon a time, these peculiarities of each people—these customs, creeds, languages—were conditions necessary for the life of humanity, in our time these same peculiarities form the chief obstacle to what is already recognized as an ideal—the brotherly union of the peoples?

And therefore the maintenance and defense of any nationality—Russian, German, French, or Anglo-Saxon, provoking the corresponding maintenance and defense not only of Hungarian, Polish, and Irish nationalities, but also of Basque, Provençal, Mordvá, Tchouvásh, and many other nationalities—serves not to harmonize and unite men but to estrange and divide them more and more from one another.

So that not the imaginary but the real patriotism which we all know, by which most people today are swayed and from which humanity suffers so severely, is not the wish for spiritual benefits for one's own people (it is impossible to desire spiritual benefits for one's own people only), but is a very definite feeling of preference for one's own people or State above all other peoples and States, and a consequent wish to get for that people or State the greatest advantages and power that can be got—things which are obtainable only at the expense of the advantages and power of other peoples or States.

It would therefore seem obvious that patriotism as a feeling is bad and harmful, and as a doctrine is stupid. For it is clear that if each people and each State considers itself the best of peoples and States, they all live in a gross and harmful delusion.

One would expect the harmfulness and irrationality of patriotism to be evident to everybody. But the surprising fact is that cultured and learned men not only do not themselves notice the harm and stupidity of patriotism, but resist every exposure of it with the greatest obstinacy and ardor (though without any rational grounds) and continue to belaud it as beneficent and elevating.

What does this mean?

Only one explanation of this amazing fact presents itself to me.

All human history from the earliest times to our own day may be considered as a movement of the consciousness both of individuals and of homogeneous groups from lower ideas to higher ones.

The whole path traveled both by individuals and by homogeneous groups may be represented as a consecutive flight of steps from the lowest, on the level of animal life, to the highest attained by the consciousness of man at a given moment of history.

Each man, like each separate homogeneous group, nation, or State, always moved and moves up this ladder of ideas. Some portions of humanity are in front, others lag far behind, others again the majority move somewhere between the most advanced and the most backward. But all, whatever stage they may have reached, are inevitably and irresistibly moving from lower to higher ideas. And always, at any given moment, both the individuals and the separate groups of people—advanced, middle, or backward—stand in three different relations to the three stages of ideas amid which they move.

Always, both for the individual and for the separate groups of people, there are the ideas of the past, which are worn out and have become strange to them and to which they cannot revert: as for instance in our Christian world, the ideas of cannibalism, universal plunder, the rape of wives, and other customs of which only a record remains.

And there are the ideas of the present, instilled into men's minds by education, by example, and by the general activity of all around them; ideas under the power of which they live at a given time: for instance, in our own day, the ideas of property, State organization, trade, utilization of domestic animals, and so on.

And there are the ideas of the future, of which some are already approaching realization and are obliging people to change their way of life and to struggle against the former ways: such ideas in our world as those of freeing the laborers, of giving equality to women, of ceasing to use flesh food, and so on; while others, though already recognized, have not yet come into practical conflict with the old forms of life: such in our times are the ideas (which we call ideals) of the extermination of violence, the arrangement of a communal system of property, of a universal religion, and of a general brotherhood of men.

And therefore every man and every homogeneous group of

men, on whatever level they may stand, having behind them the outworn remembrances of the past and before them the ideals of the future, are always in a state of struggle between the moribund ideas of the present and the ideas of the future that are coming to life. It usually happens that when an idea which has been useful and even necessary in the past becomes superfluous, that idea, after a more or less prolonged struggle, yields its place to a new idea which was till then an ideal, but which thus becomes a present idea.

But it does occur that an antiquated idea, already replaced in people's consciousness by a higher one, is of such a kind that its maintenance is profitable to those who have the greatest influence in their society. And then it happens that this antiquated idea, though it is in sharp contradiction to the whole surrounding form of life which has been altering in other respects, continues to influence people and to sway their actions. Such retention of antiquated ideas always has occurred, and still does occur, in the region of religion. And it occurs because the priests, whose profitable positions are bound up with the antiquated religious idea, purposely use their power to hold people to this antiquated idea.

The same thing occurs in the political sphere, and for similar reasons, with reference to the patriotic idea on which all arbitrary power is based. People to whom it is profitable to do so maintain that idea by artificial means though it now lacks both sense and utility. And as these people possess the most powerful means of influencing others, they are able to achieve their object.

In this, it seems to me, lies the explanation of the strange contrast between the antiquated patriotic idea and that whole drift of ideas making in a contrary direction which has already entered into the consciousness of the Christian world.

Patriotism as a feeling of exclusive love for one's own people and as a doctrine of the virtue of sacrificing one's tranquillity, one's property, and even one's life, in defense of one's own people from slaughter and outrage by their enemies, was the highest idea of the period when each nation considered it feasible and just for its own advantage to subject to slaughter and outrage the people of other nations.

But already some two thousand years ago humanity, in the person of the highest representatives of its wisdom, began to recognize the higher idea of a brotherhood of man; and that idea penetrating man's consciousness more and more, has in our time attained most varied forms of realization. Thanks to improved means of communication and to the unity of industry, of trade, of the arts, and of science, men are today so bound to one another that the danger of conquest, massacre, or outrage by a neighboring people has quite disappeared, and all peoples (the peoples, but not the governments) live together in peaceful, mutually advantageous, and friendly commercial, industrial, artistic, and scientific relations, which they have no need and no desire to disturb. One would think therefore that the antiquated feeling of patriotism—being superfluous and incompatible with the consciousness we have reached of the existence of brotherhood among men of different nationalities—should dwindle more and more until it completely disappears. Yet the very opposite of this occurs: this harmful and antiquated feeling not only continues to exist, but burns more and more fiercely.

The peoples without any reasonable ground and contrary alike to their conception of right and to their own advantage, not only sympathize with governments in their attacks on other nations, in their seizures of foreign possessions and in defending by force what they have already stolen, but even themselves demand such attacks, seizures, and defenses: are glad of them and take pride in them. The small oppressed nationalities which have fallen under the power of the great States—the Poles, Irish, Bohemians, Finns, or Armenians—resenting the patriotism of their conquerors which is the cause of their oppression, catch from them the infection of this feeling of patriotism—which has ceased to be necessary and is now obsolete, unmeaning, and harmful—and catch it to such a degree that all their activity is concentrated upon it, and though they are themselves suffering from the patriotism of the stronger nations, they are ready for the sake of patriotism to perpetrate on other peoples the very same deeds that their oppressors have perpetrated and are perpetrating on them.

This occurs because the ruling classes (including not only the actual rulers with their officials but all the classes who enjoy an exceptionally advantageous position: the capitalists, journalists, and most of the artists and scientists) can retain their position—an exceptionally advantageous one in comparison with that of the laboring masses—thanks only to the government organization which rests on patriotism. They have in their hands all the most powerful means of influencing the people, and always sedulously support patriotic feelings in themselves and in others, more especially as those feelings which uphold the government's power are those that are always best rewarded by that power.

The more patriotic an official is, the more he prospers in his career. The war produced by patriotism gives the army man a chance of promotion.

Patriotism and its resulting wars give an enormous revenue to the newspaper trade and profits to many other trades. The more every writer, teacher, and professor preaches patriotism the more secure is he in his place. The more every emperor and king is addicted to patriotism the more fame he obtains.

The ruling classes have in their hands the army, the schools, the churches, the press, and money. In the schools they kindle patriotism in the children by means of histories describing their own people as the best of all peoples and always in the right. Among adults they kindle it by spectacles, jubilees, monuments, and by a lying patriotic press. Above all they inflame patriotism by perpetrating every kind of injustice and harshness against other nations, provoking in them enmity toward their own people, and then in turn exploit that enmity to embitter their people against the foreigner.

The intensification of this terrible feeling of patriotism has gone on among the European peoples in a rapidly increasing progression, and in our time has reached the utmost limits beyond which there is no room for it to extend.

Within the memory of people not yet old an occurrence took place showing most obviously the amazing intoxication caused by patriotism among the people of Christendom.

The ruling classes of Germany excited the patriotism of the masses of their people to such a degree that, in the second half of the nineteenth century, a law was proposed in accordance with which all the men had to become soldiers: all the sons, husbands, fathers, learned men, and godly men, had to learn to murder, to become submissive slaves of those above them in military rank, and be absolutely ready to kill whomsoever they were ordered to kill; to kill men of oppressed nationalities, their own working men standing up for their rights, and even their own fathers and brothers—as was publicly proclaimed by that most impudent of potentates, William II.

That horrible measure, outraging all man's best feelings in the grossest manner, was acquiesced in without murmur by the people of Germany under the influence of patriotism. It resulted in their victory over the French. That victory excited the patriotism of Germany yet further, and by reaction that of France, Russia, and the other Powers; and the men of the European countries unresistingly submitted to the introduction of general military service—i.e., to a state of slavery involving a degree of humiliation and submission incomparably worse than any slavery of the ancient world. After this servile submission of the masses to the calls of patriotism, the audacity, cruelty, and insanity of the governments knew no bounds. A competition in the usurpation of other peoples' lands in Asia, Africa, and America began—evoked partly by whim, partly by vanity, and partly by covetousness—and was accompanied by ever greater and greater distrust and enmity between the governments.

The destruction of the inhabitants of the lands seized was accepted as a quite natural proceeding. The only question was who should be first in seizing other peoples' land and destroying the inhabitants? All the governments not only most evidently infringed, and are infringing, the elementary demands of justice in relation to the conquered peoples and in relation to one another, but they were guilty, and continue to be guilty, of every kind of cheating, swindling, bribery, fraud, spying, robbery, and murder; and the peoples not only sympathized and still sympathize with them in all this, but rejoice when it is their own government and not another government that commits such crimes.

The mutual enmity between the different peoples and States has latterly reached such amazing dimensions that, notwithstanding the fact that there is no reason why one State should attack another, everyone knows that all the governments stand with their claws out and their teeth bared, and only waiting for someone to be in trouble or become weak, in order to tear him to pieces with as little risk as possible.

All the peoples of the so-called Christian world have been reduced by patriotism to such a state of brutality that not only those who are obliged to kill or be killed desire slaughter and rejoice in murder, but all the people of Europe and America, living peaceably in their homes exposed to no danger, are at each war—thanks to easy means of communication and to the press—in the position of the spectators in a Roman circus, and like them delight in the slaughter, and raise the bloodthirsty cry, "*Pollice verso*" ["*thumbs down*"].

And not only adults, but children too, pure, wise children, rejoice, according to their nationality, when they hear that the number killed and lacerated by lyddite or other shells on some particular day was not seven hundred but a thousand Englishmen or Boers.

And parents (I know of such cases) encourage their children in such brutality.

But that is not all. Every increase in the army of one nation (and each nation, being in danger, seeks to increase its army for patriotic reasons) obliges its neighbors to increase their armies, also from patriotism, and this evokes a fresh increase by the first nation.

And the same thing occurs with fortifications and navies: one State has built ten ironclads, a neighbor builds eleven; then the first builds twelve, and so on to infinity.

"I'll pinch you." "And I'll punch your head." "And I'll stab you with a dagger." "And I'll bludgeon you." "And I'll shoot you.". . . Only bad children, drunken men, or animals, quarrel or fight so, but yet it is just what is going on among the highest representatives of the most enlightened governments, the very men who undertake to direct the education and the morality of their subjects.

The position is becoming worse and worse, and there is no stopping this descent toward evident perdition.

The one way of escape believed in by credulous people has now been closed by recent events. I refer to the Hague Conference, and to the war between England and the Transvaal which immediately followed it.

If people who think little or only superficially were able to comfort themselves with the idea that international courts of arbitration would supersede wars and ever-increasing armaments, the Hague Conference and the war that followed it demonstrated in the most palpable manner the impossibility of finding a solution of the difficulty in that way. After the Hague Conference it became obvious that as long as governments with armies exist, the termination of armaments and of wars is impossible. That an agreement should become possible it is necessary that the parties to it should *trust* each other. And in order that the Powers should trust each other they must lay down their arms, as is done by the bearers of a flag of truce when they meet for a conference.

So long as governments continue to distrust one another, and instead of disbanding or decreasing their armies always increase them in correspondence with augmentations made by their neighbors, and by means of spies watch every movement of troops, knowing that each of the Powers will attack its neighbor as soon as it sees its way to do so, no agreement is possible, and every conference is either a stupidity, or a pastime, or a fraud, or an impertinence, or all of these together. . . . The delegates met—knowing in advance that nothing would come of it—and for several weeks (during which they drew good salaries), though laughing in their sleeves, they all conscientiously pretended to be much occupied in arranging peace among the nations.

The Hague Conference, followed up as it was by the terrible bloodshed of the Transvaal War which no one attempted or is now attempting to stop, was nevertheless of some use, though not at all in the way expected of it—it was useful because it showed in the most obvious manner that the evils from which the peoples are suffering cannot be cured by governments; that governments, even if they wished to, cannot terminate either armaments or wars.

To have a reason for existing, governments must defend their people from other people's attack. But not one people wishes to attack or does attack another. And therefore governments, far from wishing for peace, carefully excite the anger of other nations against themselves. And having excited other people's anger against themselves and stirred up the patriotism of their own people, each government then assures its people that it is in danger and must be defended.

And having the power in their hands the governments can both irritate other nations and excite patriotism at home, and they carefully do both the one and the other. Nor can they do otherwise, for their existence depends on their acting thus.

If in former times governments were necessary to defend their people from other people's attacks, now on the contrary governments artificially disturb the peace that exists between the nations and provoke enmity among them.

When it was necessary to plough in order to sow, ploughing was wise, but it is evidently absurd and harmful to go on ploughing after the seed has been sown. But this is just what the governments are obliging their people to do: to infringe the unity which exists and which nothing would infringe were it not for the governments.

What really are these governments without which people think they could not exist?

There may have been a time when such governments were necessary, and when the evil of supporting a government was less than that of being defenseless against organized neighbors; but now such governments have become unnecessary and are a far greater evil than all the dangers with which they frighten their subjects.

Not only military governments but governments in general could be, I will not say useful but at least harmless, only if they consisted of immaculate, holy people, as is theoretically the case among the Chinese. But then, by the nature of their activity which consists in committing acts of violence,* governments are always composed of elements quite contrary to holiness—of the most audacious, unscrupulous, and perverted people.

A government therefore is the most dangerous organization possible, especially when it is entrusted with military power.

In the widest sense the government, including capitalists and the Press, is nothing but an organization which places the greater part of the people in the power of a smaller part who dominate them. That smaller part is subject to a yet smaller part, that again to a yet smaller, and so on, reaching at last a few people or one single man who by means of military force has power over all the rest. So that all this organization resembles a cone of which all the parts are completely in the power of those people, or that one person, who happen to be at the apex. . . .

*The word *government* is frequently used in an indefinite sense as almost equivalent to management or direction; but in the sense in which the word is used in the present article, the characteristic feature of a government is that it claims a moral right to inflict physical penalties and by its decree to make murder a good action.—Translator's note.

"But," it is usually asked, "what will there be instead of governments?"

There will be nothing. Something that has long been useless and therefore superfluous and bad will be abolished. An organ that being unnecessary has become harmful will be abolished.

"But," people generally say, "if there is no government people will violate and kill each other."

Why? Why should the abolition of the organization which arose in consequence of violence and which has been handed down from generation to generation to do violence—why should the abolition of such an organization, now devoid of use, cause people to outrage and kill one another? On the contrary, the presumption is that the abolition of the organ of violence would result in people ceasing to violate and kill one another.

Now some men are specially educated and trained to kill and to do violence to other people—there are men who are supposed to have a right to use violence, and who make use of an organization which exists for that purpose. Such deeds of violence and such killing are considered good and worthy deeds.

But then people will not be so brought up, and no one will have a right to use violence to others, and there will be no organization to do violence, and—as is natural to people of our time—violence and murder will always be considered bad actions no matter who commits them.

But should acts of violence continue to be committed even after the abolition of the governments, such acts will certainly be fewer than they are now when an organization specially devised to commit acts of violence exists, and we have a state of things in which acts of violence and murders are considered good and useful deeds.

The abolition of governments will merely rid us of an unnecessary organization which we have inherited from the past, an organization for the commission of violence and for its justification.

"But there will then be no laws, no property, no courts of justice, no police, no popular education," say people who intentionally confuse the use of violence by governments with various social activities.

The abolition of the organization of government formed to do violence does not at all involve the abolition of what is reasonable and good, and therefore not based on violence, in laws or law courts, or in property, or in police regulations, or in financial arrangements, or in popular education. On the contrary, the absence of the brutal power of government which is needed only for its own support, will facilitate a more just and reasonable social organization, needing no violence. Courts of justice, and public affairs, and popular education, will all exist to the extent to which they are really needed by the people, but in a form which will not involve the evils contained in the present form of government. Only that will be destroyed which was evil and hindered the free expression of the people's will.

But even if we assume that with the absence of governments there would be disturbances and civil strife, even then the position of the people would be better than it is at present. The position now is such that it is difficult to imagine anything worse. The people are ruined, and their ruin is becoming more and more complete. The men are all converted into war-slaves, and have from day to day to expect orders to go to kill and to be killed. What more? Are the ruined peoples to die of hunger? Even that is already beginning in Russia, in Italy, and in India. Or are the women as well as the men to go as soldiers? In the Transvaal even that has begun.

So that even if the absence of government really meant anarchy in the negative disorderly sense of that word—which is far from being the case—even then no anarchical disorder could be worse than the position to which governments have already led their peoples, and to which they are leading them.

And therefore emancipation from patriotism and the destruction of the despotism of government that rests upon it, cannot but be beneficial to mankind.

Men, bethink yourselves! For the sake of your well-being, physical and spiritual, for the sake of your brothers and sisters, pause, consider, and think of what you are doing!

Reflect, and you will understand that your foes are not the Boers, or the English, or the French, or the Germans, or the Finns, or the Russians, but that your foes—your only foes— are you yourselves, who by your patriotism maintain the governments that oppress you and make you unhappy.

They have undertaken to protect you from danger and they have brought that pseudo-protection to such a point that you have all become soldiers—slaves—and are all ruined, or are being ruined more and more, and at any moment may and should expect that the tight-stretched cord will snap and a horrible slaughter of you and your children will commence.

And however great that slaughter may be and however that conflict may end the same state of things will continue. In the same way and with yet greater intensity, the governments will arm, and ruin, and pervert you and your children, and no one will help you to stop it or prevent it if you do not help yourselves.

There is only one kind of help possible—the abolition of that terrible cone of violence which enables the person or persons who succeed in seizing the apex to have power over all the rest, and to hold that power the more firmly the more cruel and inhuman they are, as we see by the cases of Napoleons, Nicholas I, Bismarck, Chamberlain, Rhodes, and our Russian Dictators who rule the people in the Tsar's name.

There is only one way to destroy the binding together of this cone—it is by shaking off the hypnotism of patriotism.

Understand that you yourselves cause all the evils from which you suffer, by yielding to the suggestions by which emperors, kings, members of Parliament, governors, officers, capitalists, priests, authors, artists, and all who need this fraud of patriotism in order to live upon your labor, deceive you!

Whoever you may be—Frenchman, Russian, Pole, Englishman, Irishman, or Bohemian—understand that all your real human interests, whatever they may be—agricultural, industrial, commercial, artistic, or scientific—as well as your pleasures and joys, in no way run counter to the interests of other peoples or States, and that you are united with the folk of other lands by mutual cooperation, by interchange of services, by the joy of wide brotherly intercourse, and by the interchange not merely of goods but also of thoughts and feelings.

Understand that the question as to whether your government or another manages to seize Wei hai wei, Port Arthur, or Cuba does not affect you, or rather that every such seizure made by your government injures you by inevitably bringing in its train all sorts of pressure by your government to force you to take part in the robbery and violence by which alone such seizures are made, or can be retained when made. Understand that your life can in no way be bettered by Alsace becoming German or French and Ireland or Poland being free or en-slaved—whoever holds them. You are free to live where you will, even if you be an Alsatian, an Irishman, or a Pole. Understand too, that by stirring up patriotism you will only make the case worse, for the subjection in which your people are kept has resulted simply from the struggle between patrio-tisms, and every manifestation of patriotism in one nation provokes a corresponding reaction in another. Understand that salvation from your woes is only possible when you free your-self from the obsolete idea of patriotism and from the obedi-ence to governments that is based upon it, and when you boldly enter into the region of that higher idea, the brotherly union of the peoples, which has long since come to life and from all sides is calling you to itself.

If people would but understand that they are not the sons of some fatherland or other, nor of governments, but are sons of God and can therefore neither be slaves nor enemies one to another—those insane, unnecessary, worn-out, pernicious orga-nizations called governments would cease, and with them all the sufferings, violations, humiliations, and crimes which they occasion.

7 Essentials of Anarchism

DAVID THOREAU WIECK

David Wieck (1921—), now a philosophy professor at Rensselaer Polytechnic Institute, was editor and the major writer for Resistance, *one of the best anarchist periodicals. Published from 1947 to 1954, it was a continuation of* Why? *(1942–47). It was the organ of the now defunct Resistance Group, which was formed after World War II to oppose war and militarism while advocating anarchism. Its members urged and practiced draft resistance long before war in Vietnam made such actions relatively common. This essay is representative of recent anarchist philosophy; for other examples one might well read some of the work of Paul Goodman, also a member of the Resistance Group and author of the last piece in this volume.*

Anarchy, as a political ideal, means simply "no government." There are, therefore, a number of theories about anarchy, all accurately labeled "anarchism." This leads on the one hand to confusion, but on the other hand to a free and presumably valuable conflict of ideas. So we shall not worry over it here. We shall confine ourselves to the essentials of what the writer considers the best in anarchist thought, and arbitrarily call it "anarchism." . . .

THE LIFE WE LIVE

Anarchism begins by evaluating the society we live in—our "way of life." In this life we find too much misery and unhap-

From *Resistance*, XI:1 (August 1953), 4–7, 18.

piness, too much destruction, too little fulfillment of the potentialities of human beings.

First, there are the gross evils that everyone perceives: the
waste, the destruction, the restrictions. Our nation is involved
in endless wars, the government conscripts our young men,
wealth is destroyed. Our natural riches, our scientific genius,
are not shared with the impoverished nations of the world, but
are the means of control and exploitation. Now, in the climate
of permanent war, a great cloud of prohibition and fear is
darkening the face of our people, and citizens fearful of being
silenced are beginning to learn the dismal art of silence.

Thinking people are aware, too, that after a dozen years of
high prosperity, millions still live on the borderline of poverty.
They know a little of what it means in America to belong to a
dark-skinned race. It is easy to see that only a minority of
Americans can "succeed," while the greater number are condemned to lifelong, futile pursuit of the goals of wealth and
social status they have been educated to aspire to.

The truth is that the wealth, the position, the standard of
living we have learned to strive for, do not yield deep satisfaction—they are joyless and even boring. The successful man
feels a dissatisfaction he tries to resolve by renewed struggle to
achieve greater heights. In our emphasis on wealth and status,
we squeeze out everything irrelevant to these goals, everything
that could possibly be worthy of our effort, and rewarding.

We all know that work is dominated by motives of profit—
but this is not the worst. It is absolutely dominated by motives
of *consumption:* as profits, or wages, or (in "welfare" theories)
quantity of social production. To this aim all our scientific
endeavor, all our ingenuity of organization, is attuned. But
man is not—need it be said?—merely a *consumer,* he is a
worker. As a worker he is now only a machine-tender, a passive
instrument of industries geared to production of quantity. The
deterioration of the quality of goods is a painful, if minor,
consequence of this one-sided economy; the debasement of
work in a society dedicated to economic progress is an irony
and a disaster.

(To be sure, the mechanized industrial worker is still chiefly a symbol, and a shadow-before, not yet an omnipresent fact. But when we consider the plight of the white-collar worker, lacking even the producer's claim to dignity, we see how pervasive the debasement of work is already.)

In our society, too, we take it for granted that we should be strangers to each other—strangers who work together, and "deal" with each other, by the media of authority and money-exchange. We miss, hardly aware of our loss, the qualities of social warmth, of fraternal rivalry and cooperation—we miss these satisfactions and the strength they would give us.

We take it for granted that a small number of people, more or less talented, shall make—one would hardly say "create"—under the usual consumption-oriented conditions of the market, our "works of art," our "entertainment," while the rest of us are spectators.

And we are also a people who, in grave conflict within ourselves, have created all manner of crippling make-shifts to reconcile, with the life-goals our society teaches us, with the demands for conformity made upon us, our half-perceived but real yearnings for love, for self-respect, for friendships, for creative activities. Or rather, not reconciled the two forces, but reconciled ourselves to heavy deprivations.

Now, we must praise our country for its marvelous productive techniques, its medical miracles, the high development of scientific knowledge. We have, as few societies have ever had, the basis for living. But there is still—except for a very few—nothing but existence, an unworthy survival.

It is the purpose of anarchism to look beyond survival—to look at what must be done if we are to achieve a worthy and noble life.

THE LIMITS AND FAILURES OF REFORM

How can these problems be met? The obvious way, the one continually tried by good-intentioned people, is to attack each problem separately. We are plagued by war—so we look for ways to achieve peace. Poverty and gross inequality are unjust and destructive—the treatment of law-breakers is a scandal to a civilized country—our educational systems make the many literate, but educate very few—and so, on these and many other fronts, men and women are working to undo the evils.

A right beginning! But it does not turn out well, and failure to pay frank attention to the results, and the reasons for the results, leaves many good-hearted people fixed in dead-ends.

In certain cases, like war, the evil stubbornly resists every effort to abolish it, or even limit it.

In other cases the evil can be modified, but its most destructive features persist. Thus, prison reform can eliminate certain brutalities, but imprisonment, no matter how modified, destroys the best qualities in a man. Or, the conditions of labor in industry are improved—the worker is protected against injury, discharge and humiliation—but the work does not, by becoming less inhumane, become human. Or, the living standards of workers are raised—but still the worker must sell his labor-power, still he is only an instrument, a hand, whose mind and inventiveness are not wanted. Nor does "economic security" transform a lonely, frightened citizen into a human being.

Or a third thing occurs: the reform can be achieved, but only by adding to the bureaucratic structure of society. Such has been the destiny of the labor movement. And bureaucracy is the deliberate—and only possible—method of government to cope with economic destitution in old age, with the reckless exploitation of natural resources, with the economic piracy of monopolists—and most of the targets of the New Deal.

(To illustrate the meaning of bureaucracy, consider the coal mine safety problem. In the youth of the union, state mine-inspection, plus the militant pressure of local miner-leaders, worked adequately wherever local vitality existed. Centralization of the union destroyed this vitality. To counterbalance the mine-owner-dominated safety bureaus, a federal system of inspection has been created. The gain is unequivocal; but multiplication of authority cannot meet the need. The persons who can and should guard their safety, and make it primary rather than an afterthought, are the miners. But they have abdicated their power.)

Undeniably, these many efforts respond to real needs, and their achievements are not negligible. But still the quality of life does not improve. Almost invariably, the evil is beyond reach; or it can be touched only at the edges; or it can be modified only by increasing the evil of bureaucracy. Meanwhile, the influence of war, the influence of habituation to our way of life, are giving our society an increasingly ugly tone.

WHY THE ANARCHIST PROPOSALS ARE SO EXTREME

If we look at the history of each reform-effort, we can see that neither lack of good will, nor ignorance, has defeated or limited them. Reform has failed because each of these evils fulfills an essential function in our society (or is bound up with an essential function), and none can be arbitrarily ripped out of the total pattern. In the best cases, the evils can be mitigated only by the pyramiding of bureaucracy. In the worst cases, not even this much relief is possible.

How could the unequal property system be upheld without police and prisons? How can capitalist exploitation be mitigated, if not by the superimposition of bureaucracy? How could there be community when people are competing desperately with each other, when we are frightened of each other, hostile toward each other? How can our lives as workers become different, while consumption and war remain the dominant motives? How can there be war, and no centralized government? How centralized government, and no war? The list could be extended almost indefinitely. These are the dilemmas of reform.

Our society does change constantly, of course—but always it turns on the poles of power, war, the State. It becomes more bureaucratic or less, more warlike or less, more restricting or less—there can be all the stages from Capitalism to State

Communism, from limited democracy to totalitarianism. These variations can mean the difference between tolerable and intolerable existence. But they do not allow, in the best of them, for the growth and development of Man. For the great majority of people, there is no life, merely laborious survival.

In order to give a new tone to our society, a new quality to our life, we must change the central principles of our society— we must learn how to live socially, and work together, without the profit-and-power motive; without a monopoly property-system; without centralized political authority; without war. This is why the anarchist proposals are so extreme, so sweeping; and why anything short of them brings disappointment, only superficial change.

(We do not contend, of course, that reforms are worthless, when they relieve suffering, or increase liberty. When these ends can be achieved only by bureaucratic methods, however, they do indirect damage which their positive value may not balance. How these specific choices are to be made, in terms of our values, is too complicated to consider here.)

THE HYPOTHESIS OF FREEDOM

Anarchists, anarchists alone, propose to reorganize our common life without the crippling destructive principles of power, monopoly-property, and war.

The principle which anarchists propose to substitute is Freedom—but freedom in a sense quite different from its debasement in the wars of propaganda. We contend that men need to be free of restriction in order to grow to the limit of their powers—and that when these powers are released from inhibition, entirely new solutions to our economic, political, and social problems will be possible.

Our anarchist philosophers have emphasized different facets of our unutilized "human resources":

1. Man tends to be rational, to be able to recognize his problems and solve them. A false education, from infancy to

adulthood, and the "positive institutions" by which society has tried to preserve order and morality among a bewildered population, have crippled these powers. Let men be free, from the first, encouraged to discover their own abilities and own interests, let them be ungoverned, and they will tend to have "right opinions."

(In the false education of today, the suppression and distortion of sensual pleasure certainly plays a dynamic role. I think it remains moot whether it plays a decisive *initiating* role—and will therefore be a special problem in achieving freedom—or is a reflex of social unhappiness, inhibition of sociality, and other factors. In either case, its crippling influences make the sexual mores, both here and now and in respect to a free society, a natural major concern of anarchists.)

2. The self-interests of people clash, but we need not dread this clash. It is destructive now because people submit to others, because they acknowledge Power and Authority. It can be productive, it will lead men beyond anything the isolated individual could possibly conceive of—and Authority is just such an isolated individual—but only if men are unashamedly themselves, not possessed by Ideas, Gods, Authorities, or Neuroses.

3. Men possess a natural tendency to solidarity, to cooperation. This tendency our social institutions check and even suppress. Let men rid themselves of these constraints, and we will come into our biological heritage of mutual aid.

(These are the major lessons to be drawn from Godwin, Stirner, and Kropotkin.)

Reason, fraternal conflict, mutual aid—these powers of men, stifled in our lives today, can be the principles, the heart of a new society. Men must be free of the control and restrictions of economic and legal authorities, free of coercion to conformity: but these constraints exist because men *accept* them, so they must be *willing* to be free. This is the hypothesis of freedom.

Let men be free, and then the problems of economics and politics can find good solutions. No longer need our industries be owned monopolistically by corporations or government—the practice of voluntary cooperation, the principle of equality, will allow new kinds of organization. Released from cramping monopoly ownership, our engineering and managerial ingenuity will find ways to balance our interests as consumers and as workers. Our political life will no more be centralized in national government, and men and women will gain sovereignty over their destinies. The individual can be liberated from demands for conformity—we will need no more prisons—and so on through a host of "social problems" which remain unsolvable so long as the fundamental principles of the society are unchanged.

(Oh, yes! the solutions will tax our ingenuity. But at last they will be, in principle, possible, and the freedom of communities and groups to try even the most extreme experiments should accelerate the discovery of the best solutions.)

"Man Is Perfectible"

Nothing less than Paradise!—so it must seem to those afraid of bold dreams. Certainly we cannot fail to confirm the charge that anarchists are visionaries who solve all imaginable problems—in the imagination. For no society like we suggest has ever existed.

No! On the contrary! The vision is modest; it is only because we are habituated to a meager life, only because we have timidly accepted the traditions of capitalist-militarist society, that freedom appears fantastic. Once achieved, it will doubtless seem like no more than a stage in human progress.

Nevertheless, facts are facts, and freedom is only a hypothesis. Not that anarchists have not, whenever possible, grasped opportunities to make the hypothesis real—but then, as in Russia and Spain, this dangerous idea has been crushed before it could show its merits (or, if we are wrong, its demerits).

We believe it conforms to the best knowledge about men and society; we believe each of us can feel in ourselves the needs, the desires, the potentialities to which it answers. "Man is perfectible"—which means "in our societies we have not begun to explore the potentialities of man."

History is not, as man used to hope, marching us toward our freedom. We claim only this: we see in man the potentiality of living in freedom; we know there are times, now and then, when social conflicts create the demand for liberty, for equality, for justice, and moments when the grip of the past is loosened and choice becomes possible. At such times, can the desire for freedom, the love of freedom, be evoked in people by anarchists? This is our hope.

The present is not a time when men feel an excess of power, or ideals seem possible of realization. Our time is permeated by despair and deadness of spirit. To submit to this spirit is simply to confirm it. Those who are able to perceive that this is a time of degradation, and not an inevitable expression of man's nature, have a responsibility to hold before their countrymen an image of what men *may* be, if we gain our freedom and humanity.

The Necessary Vagueness of Our Conception of Freedom

A true description of freedom, of a free society, is unfortunately very indefinite, and does not at all compare with the utopian blueprints it is so easy to whip up. If someone outlines a scheme of social organization and says, "This is freedom," he is not speaking of freedom. Men can be free if they choose, by their own actions, the social organization they will live within; and unless, of course, the organizations they choose permit them to retain their freedom. (Man is not born free—even in a free society; it is a quality he must earn.)

We can, as have particular schools of anarchism, work out in detail our vision of a free society. If we never forget that these Utopias are not "the only practical freedom," they provide a way to test imaginatively the hypothesis of freedom. When opportunities finally arise, then we shall have to think through the first acts of freedom; but first people must gain the will to be free. What marvelous arrangements they will invent then, it is hardly worth the trouble to try to guess.

WHY FREEDOM MUST BE EARNED

Freedom, we have said, cannot be won by gradual reform, for the evils are interdependent, the system is a whole. Freedom must be achieved integrally, but how?

"This life will not be thrust upon us, we shall have to earn it."

Because our idea of Freedom is so radical, most persons slightly acquainted with anarchism never grasp it. They persist in the illusion that we, like the political parties, have a *plan* which we seek the power to *impose*. We do not have a plan, nor anything to impose. We have an Idea, which can be realized only when, and if, people desire it and will it.

When we say people can become free only by will, only by acts of freedom, we are not juggling words. We mean that freedom is not merely the absence of restrictions—it is responsibility, choice, and the free assumption of social obligations.

(Herbert Read has suggested reasons for using "liberty" to denote the absence of restrictions, and "freedom" to denote the positive qualities of responsible sociality, etc. Following these definitions, the hypothesis here is that, without Freedom, liberty can endure only at the price of social rigidity, as in the less authoritarian primitive societies. For Western Man, with his vast stores of knowledge and traditions of "curiosity," such a choice, were it desirable, is hardly possible.)

In the achievement of freedom, the conscious will to freedom is obviously not the only factor—but it is the essential factor. When people begin to lose faith in the old order and a revolution occurs, communalistic, democratic institutions invariably spring up to perform the functions of the fallen institutions. As at all times, the work of anarchists is to show people how they can extend their freedom—because if they do not, authority speedily reconstitutes itself.

Again and again, revolutionary thinkers have made the mistake of believing that a revolution can be saved if they gain power, and impose the "right" institutions. But no institutions can complete the revolution, unless freely chosen by the people. The tragic alternative is the tyrannical revolutionary bureaucracy.

Progress toward freedom consists of the awakening of desire for freedom in the apathetic masses. It consists in *resisting and undermining even the revolutionary institutions,* when they do not yet represent the free actions of the people. Even theoretically, this idea is difficult; but by it, we can understand why revolutions have all turned out so badly, *why a revolution is desirable only if it can lead toward freedom.* People who are deprived of masters, but do not desire to be free, have never had difficulty in finding new masters.

THE SLOW PROGRESS OF ANARCHISM

We have certainly left "reality" far behind—and though it is not fashionable, it is not a bad thing. But we can act only in the present. To achieve freedom, "people" must desire and will it; but we know perfectly that people have not the slightest inclination to do so, yet. That people are human, or proletarians, or intellectuals, gives them no automatic impulse toward freedom. It is nice to talk of "the universal yearning to be free"—but this means only, "people do not like to feel oppressed and restricted"; it certainly cannot mean that they yearn to make choices and exercise the responsibilities of free men. To be free—not merely to escape oppression—is a potentiality of man, the condition, we think, of man's nobility; not given, only earned.

The anarchist idea of freedom is a very serious one; it implies a view of life that people do not yet have. This is why we cannot—must not—hawk our ideological wares in the manner of the political parties or the hucksters of thought. If we were foolish enough, we could cry out that we are for liberty, and Americans are supposed to believe in liberty, so "Do as we say." It is always possible to draw a crowd in this way. (To be sure, it would be nice to draw a crowd just once in a while!) But anarchism is a serious idea, and misrepresentation is its death.

When there are more of us, and we can stop merely talking about it and can begin here and there to give practical demonstrations of freedom, then, we believe, freedom has such power that our propaganda will be easily made and persuasive. Until then, anarchism must progress slowly, and nothing so much as patience is required.

THE REALIZATION OF FREEDOM

In short, anarchism is a philosophy based on the premise that men need freedom in order to solve urgent social problems, and begin to realize their potentialities for happiness and creativity. Anarchists initiate their practical actions by looking squarely at the time and place they live in, and deciding what can be done *now* to forward their goal: to find the next step to be taken, to take it, and encourage others to move ahead.

The step to be taken now, we believe, is to keep alive the idea of freedom, and the desires it is meant to serve; to live and work with people and act toward social institutions in the ways which will grant us the nearest approach to the humanity of which we dream; to come together in the solidarity of anarchists to invent actions together. In these ways, if we are inventive, we can introduce into our neighbors' lives the idea and practice of freedom.

8 The Impossibilities of Anarchism

GEORGE BERNARD SHAW

George Bernard Shaw (1856–1950) possessed magnificent wit and command of language which made him unsurpassed as a dramatist and literary critic; it also made him a formidable spokesman for socialism, to which for the best part of a century he devoted much of his great talent. After a relatively brief flirtation with anarchism, Shaw became one of the major figures in the Fabian Society, an organization of British intellectuals advocating moderate evolutionary socialism. In the first part (omitted here) of this essay, he criticizes individualist anarchism, as advocated by the American, Benjamin Tucker. His discussion of "Communism" refers to a form of anarchism then called communist, with Peter Kropotkin's ideas the main example. By "Social-Democracy" Shaw means democratic socialism, such as that urged by the Fabian Society.

The main difficulty in criticizing Kropotkine lies in the fact that, in the distribution of generally needed labor products, his Communism is finally cheap and expedient, whereas Mr. Tucker's Individualism, in the same department, is finally extravagant and impossible. Even under the most perfect Social-Democracy we should, without Communism, still be living like hogs, except that each hog would get his fair share of grub. High as that ideal must seem to anyone who complacently accepts the present social order, it is hardly high enough to satisfy a man in whom the social instinct is well developed. So long as vast quantities of labor have to be expended in weighing and measuring each man's earned share

Fabian Tract No. 45 (London: The Fabian Society, 1893), pp. 12–27. The text, written in 1891, has been condensed. Reprinted by permission of The Society of Authors, for the Bernard Shaw Estate.

of this and that commodity—in watching, spying, policing, and punishing in order to prevent Tom getting a crumb of bread more or Dick a spoonful of milk less than he has a voucher for, so long will the difference between Unsocialism and Socialism be only the difference between unscientific and scientific hoggishness. I do not desire to underrate the vastness of that difference. Whilst we are hogs, let us at least be well-fed, healthy, reciprocally useful hogs, instead of well, instead of the sort we are at present. But we shall not have any great reason to stand on the dignity of our humanity until a just distribution of the loaves and fishes becomes perfectly spontaneous, and the great effort and expense of a legal distribution, however just, is saved. For my own part, I seek the establishment of a state of society in which I shall not be bothered with a ridiculous pocketful of coppers, nor have to waste my time in perplexing arithmetical exchanges of them with booking clerks, bus conductors, shopmen, and other superfluous persons before I can get what I need. I aspire to live in a community which shall be at least capable of averaging the transactions between us well enough to ascertain how much work I am to do for it in return for the right to take what I want of the commoner necessaries and conveniences of life. The saving of friction by such an arrangement may be guessed from the curious fact that only specialists in sociology are conscious of the numerous instances in which we are today forced to adopt it by the very absurdity of the alternative. Most people will tell you that Communism is known only in this country as a visionary project advocated by a handful of amiable cranks. Then they will stroll off across the common bridge, along the common embankment, by the light of the common gas lamp shining alike on the just and the unjust, up the common street, and into the common Trafalgar Square, where, on the smallest hint on their part that Communism is to be tolerated for an instant in a civilized country, they will be handily bludgeoned by the common policeman, and haled off to the common gaol. When you suggest to these people that the application of Communism to the bread supply is only an extension, involving no new principle, of its application to street lighting, they are bewildered. Instead of picturing the Communist man going to the common store, and thence taking his bread home with him, they instinctively imagine him bursting obstreperously into his neighbor's house and snatching the bread off his table on the "as much mine as yours" principle—which, however, has an equally sharp edge for the thief's throat in the form "as much yours as mine." In fact, the average Englishman is only capable of understanding Communism when it is explained as a state of things under which everything is paid for out of the taxes, and taxes are paid in labor. And even then he will sometimes say, "How about the brainwork?" and begin the usual novice's criticism of Socialism in general.

Now a Communist Anarchist may demur to such a definition of Communism as I have just given; for it is evident that if there are to be taxes, there must be some authority to collect those taxes. I will not insist on the odious word taxes; but I submit that if any article—bread, for instance—be communized, by which I mean that there shall be public stores of bread, sufficient to satisfy everybody, to which all may come and take what they need without question or payment, wheat must be grown, mills must grind, and bakers must sweat daily in order to keep up the supply. Obviously, therefore, the common bread store will become bankrupt unless every consumer of the bread contributes to its support as much labor as the bread he consumes costs to produce. Communism or no Communism, he must pay or else leave somebody else to pay for him. Communism will cheapen bread for him—will save him the cost of scales and weights, coin, bookkeepers, counter-hands, policemen, and other expenses of private property; but it will not do away with the cost of the bread and the store. Now supposing that voluntary cooperation and public spirit prove equal to the task of elaborately organizing the farming, milling, and baking industries for the production of bread, how will these voluntary cooperators recover the cost of their operations from the public who are to consume their bread? If they are given powers to collect the cost from the public, and to enforce their demands by punishing nonpayers for their dishonesty, then they at once become a State department levying a tax for public purposes; and the Communism of the bread supply becomes no more Anarchistic than our present Communistic supply of street lighting is Anarchistic. Unless the taxation is voluntary—unless the bread consumer is free to refuse payment without incurring any penalty save the reproaches of his conscience and his neighbors, the Anarchist ideal will remain unattained. Now the pressure of conscience and public opinion is by no means to be slighted. Millions of men and women, without any legal compulsion whatever, pay for the support of institutions of all sorts, from churches to tall hats, simply out of their need for standing well with their neighbors. But observe, this compulsion of public opinion derives most of its force from the difficulty of getting the wherewithal to buy bread without a reputation for respectability. Under Communism a man could snap his fingers at public opinion without starving for it. Besides, public opinion cannot for a moment be relied upon as a force which operates uniformly as a compulsion upon men to act morally. Its operation is for all practical purposes quite arbitrary, and is as often immoral as moral. It is just as hostile to the reformer as to the criminal. It hangs Anarchists and worships Nitrate Kings. It insists on a man wearing a tall hat and going to church, on his marrying the woman he lives with, and on his pretending to believe whatever the rest pretend to believe; and it enforces these ordinances in a sufficient majority of cases without help from the law: its tyranny, in fact, being so crushing that its little finger is often found to be thicker than the law's loins. . . .

Kropotkine, too optimistically, as I think, disposes of the average man by attributing his unsocialism to the pressure of the corrupt system under which he groans. Remove that pressure, and he will think rightly, says Kropotkine. But if the natural man be indeed social as well as gregarious, how did the corruption and oppression under which he groans ever arise? Could the institution of property as we know it ever have come into existence unless nearly every man had been, not merely willing, but openly and shamelessly eager to quarter himself idly on the labor of his fellows, and to domineer over them whenever the mysterious workings of economic law enabled him to do so? It is useless to think of man as a fallen angel. If the fallacies of absolute morality are to be admitted in the discussion at all, he must be considered rather as an obstinate and selfish devil, who is being slowly forced by the iron tyranny of Nature to recognize that in disregarding his neighbor's happiness he is taking the surest way to sacrifice his own. And under the present system he never can learn that lesson thoroughly, because he is an inveterate gambler, and knows that the present system gives him a chance, at odds of a hundred thousand to one or so against him, of becoming a millionaire, a condition which is to him the summit of earthly bliss, as from it he will be able to look down upon those who formerly bullied and patronized him. All this may sound harsh, especially to those who know how wholesomely real is the workman's knowledge of life compared to that of the gentleman, and how much more genuinely sympathetic he is in consequence. Indeed, it is obvious that if four-fifths of the population were habitually to do the utter worst in the way of selfishness that the present system invites them to do, society would not stand the strain for six weeks. So far, we can claim to be better than our institutions. But the fact that we are too good for complete Unsocialism by no means proves that we are good enough for Communism. The practical question remains, Could men trained under our present system be trusted to pay for their food scrupulously if they could take it for nothing with impunity? Clearly, if they did not so pay, Anarchist Communism would be bankrupt in two days. The answer is that all the evils against which Anarchism is directed are caused by men taking advantage of the institution of property to do this very thing— seize their subsistence without working for it. What reason is there for doubting that they would attempt to take exactly the same advantage of Anarchist Communism? And what reason is there to doubt that the community, finding its bread store bankrupt, would instantly pitch its Anarchism to the four winds, and come down on the defaulters with the strong hand of a law to make them pay, just as they are now compelled to pay their Income Tax? I submit, then, to our Communist Anarchist friends that Communism requires either external compulsion to labor, or else a social morality which the evils of existing society shew that we have failed as yet to attain. I do not deny the possibility of the final attainment of that degree of moralization, but I contend that the path to it lies through a transition system which, instead of offering fresh opportunities to men of getting their living idly, will destroy those opportunities altogether, and wean us from the habit of regarding such an anomaly as possible, much less honorable.

It must not be supposed that the economic difficulties which I pointed out as fatal to Individualist Anarchism are entirely removed by Communism. It is true that if all the bread and coal in the country were thrown into a common store from which each man could take as much as he wanted whenever he pleased without direct payment, then no man could gain any advantage over his fellows from the fact that some farms and some coal-mines are better than others. And if every man could step into a train and travel whither he would without a ticket, no individual could speculate in the difference between the traffic from Charing Cross to the Mansion House and that from Ryde to Ventnor. One of the great advantages of Communism will undoubtedly be that huge masses of economic rent will be socialized by it automatically. All rent arising from the value of commodities in general use which can be produced, consumed, and replaced at the will of man to the full extent to which they are wanted, can be made rent free by communizing them. But there must remain outside this solution, first, the things which are not in sufficiently general use to be communized at all; second, things of which an unlimited free supply might prove a nuisance, such as gin or printing; and third, things for which the demand exceeds the supply. The last is the instance in which the rent difficulty recurs. . . .

One practical point more requires a word; and that is the difficulty of communizing any branch of distribution without first collectivizing it. For instance, we might easily communize the postal service by simply announcing that in future letters would be carried without stamps just as they now are with them, the cost being thrown entirely upon imperial taxation. But if the postal service were, like most of our distributive business, in the hands of thousands of competing private traders, no such change would be directly possible. Communism must grow out of Collectivism, not out of anarchic private enterprise. That is to say, it cannot grow directly out of the present system.

But must the transition system therefore be a system of despotic coercion? If so, it will be wrecked by the intense impulse of men to escape from the domination of their own kind. . . . No modern nation, if deprived of personal liberty or national antonomy, would stop to think of its economic position. Establish a form of Socialism which shall deprive the people of their sense of personal liberty; and, though it double their rations and halve their working hours, they will begin to conspire against it before it is a year old. We only disapprove of monopolists: we *hate* masters.

Then, since we are too dishonest for Communism without taxation or compulsory labor, and too insubordinate to tolerate task work under personal compulsion, how can we order the transition so as to introduce just distribution without Communism, and maintain the incentive to labor without mastership? The answer is by Democracy. And now, having taken a positive attitude at last, I must give up criticizing the Anarchists, and defend Democracy against *their* criticisms.

. . . Mr. Tucker, on the ground that "it has ever been the tendency of power to add to itself, to enlarge its sphere, to encroach beyond the limits set for it," admits no alternative to the total subjection of the individual, except the total abolition of the State. If matters really could and did come to that I am afraid the individual would have to go under in any case; for the total abolition of the State in this sense means the total abolition of the collective force of Society, to abolish which it would be necessary to abolish Society itself. . . . [People could be completely separated from one another, but they] would soon reassociate; and the moment they did so, goodbye to the sovereignty of the individual. If the majority believed in an angry and jealous God, then, State or no State, they would not permit an individual to offend that God and bring down his wrath upon them: they would rather stone and burn the individual in propitiation. They would not suffer the individual to go naked among them; and if he clothed himself in an unusual way which struck them as being ridiculous or scandalous, they would laugh at him; refuse him admission to their feasts; object to be seen talking with him in the streets; and perhaps lock him up as a lunatic. They would not allow him to neglect sanitary precautions which they believed essential to their own immunity from zymotic disease. If the family were established among them as it is established among us, they would not suffer him to intermarry within certain degrees of kinship. Their demand would so rule the market that in most places he would find no commodities in the shops except those preferred by a majority of the customers; no schools except those conducted in accordance with the ideas of the majority of parents; no experienced doctors except those whose qualifications inspired confidence in a whole circle of patients. This is not "the coming slavery" of Social-Democracy: it is the slavery already come. What is more, there is nothing in the most elaborately negative practical program yet put forward by Anarchism that offers the slightest mitigation of it. That in comparison with ideal irresponsible absolute liberty it is slavery, cannot be denied. But in comparison with the slavery of Robinson Crusoe, which is the most Anarchistic alternative Nature, our taskmistress, allows us, it is pardonably described as "freedom." Robinson Crusoe, in fact, is always willing to exchange his unlimited rights and puny powers for the curtailed rights and relatively immense powers of the "slave" of majorities. For if the individual chooses, as in most cases he will, to believe and worship as his fellows do, he finds temples built and services organized at a cost to himself which he hardly feels. The clothes, the food, the furniture which he is most likely to prefer are ready for him in the shops; the schools in which his children can be taught what their fellow citizens expect them to know are within fifteen minutes' walk of his door; and the red lamp of the most approved pattern of doctor shines reassuringly at the corner of the street. He is free to live with the women of his family without suspicion or scandal; and if he is not free to marry them, what does that matter to him, since he does not wish to marry them? And so happy man be his dole, in spite of his slavery.

"Yes," cries some eccentric individual; "but all this is untrue of me. I want to marry my deceased wife's sister. I am prepared to prove that your authorized system of medicine is nothing but a debased survival of witchcraft. Your schools are machines for forcing spurious learning on children in order that your universities may stamp them as educated men when they have finally lost all power to think for themselves. The tall silk hats and starched linen shirts which you force me to wear, and without which I cannot successfully practice as a physician, clergyman, schoolmaster, lawyer, or merchant, are inconvenient, unsanitary, ugly, pompous, and offensive. Your temples are devoted to a God in whom I do not believe; and even if I did believe in him I should still regard your popular forms of worship as only redeemed from gross superstition by their obvious insincerity. Science teaches me that my proper food is good bread and good fruit: your boasted food supply offers me cows and pigs instead. Your care for my health consists in tapping the common sewer, with its deadly typhoid gases, into my basin, besides discharging its contents into the river, which is my natural bath and fountain. Under color of protecting my person and property you forcibly take my money to support an army of soldiers and policemen for the execution of barbarous and detestable laws; for the waging of wars which I abhor; and for the subjection of my person to those legal rights of property which compel me to sell myself for a wage to a class the maintenance of which I hold to be the greatest evil of our time. Your tyranny makes my very individuality a hindrance to me: I am outdone and outbred by the mediocre, the docile, the time-serving. Evolution under such conditions means degeneracy: therefore I demand the abolition of all these officious compulsions, and proclaim myself an Anarchist."

The proclamation is not surprising under the circumstances; but it does not mend the matter in the least, nor would it if every person were to repeat it with enthusiasm, and the whole people to fly to arms for Anarchism. The majority cannot help its tyranny even if it would. The giant Winkelmeier must have found our doorways inconvenient, just as men of five feet or less find the slope of the floor in a theater not sufficiently steep to enable them to see over the heads of those in front. But whilst the average height of a man is 5 ft. 8 in., there is no redress for such grievances. Builders will accommodate doors and floors to the majority, and not to the minority. For since either the majority or the minority must be incommoded, evidently the more powerful must have its way. There may be no indisputable reason why it ought; and any clever Tory can give excellent reasons why it ought not; but the fact remains that it will, whether it ought or not. And this is what really settles the question as between democratic majorities and minorities. Where their interests conflict, the weaker side must go to the wall, because, as the evil involved is no greater than that of the stronger going to the wall,* the majority is not restrained by any scruple from compelling the weaker to give way.

In practice, this does not involve either the absolute power of majorities, or "the infallibility of the odd man." There are some matters in which the course preferred by the minority in no way obstructs that preferred by the majority. There are many more in which the obstruction is easier to bear than the cost of suppressing it. For it costs something to suppress even a minority of one. The commonest example of that minority is the lunatic with a delusion; yet it is found quite safe to enter-

---

*The evil is decidedly *less* if the calculation proceeds by the popular method of always estimating an evil suffered by a hundred persons as a hundred times as great as the same evil suffered by only one. This, however, is absurd. A hundred starving men are not a hundred times as hungry as one starving man, any more than a hundred five-foot-eight men are each five hundred and sixty-six feet eight inches high. But they are a hundred times as strong a political force. Though the evil may not be cumulative, the power to resist it is.

tain dozens of delusions, and be generally an extremely selfish and troublesome idiot, in spite of the power of majorities; for until you go so far that it clearly costs less to lock you up than to leave you at large, the majority will not take the trouble to set itself in action against you. Thus a minimum of individual liberty is secured, under any system, to the smallest minority. It is true that as minorities grow, they sometimes, in forfeiting the protection of insignificance, lose more in immunity than they gain in numbers; so that probably the weakest minority is not the smallest, but rather that which is too large to be disregarded and too weak to be feared; but before and after that dangerous point is weathered, minorities wield considerable power. The notion that they are ciphers because the majority could vanquish them in a trial of strength leaves out of account the damage they could inflict on the victors during the struggle. . . . But it is not often that a peremptory question arises between a majority and minority of a whole nation. In most matters only a fragment of the nation has any interest one way or the other; and the same man who is in a majority on one question is in a minority on another, and so learns by experience that minorities have "rights" which must be attended to. Minorities, too, as in the case of the Irish Party in the English Parliament, occasionally hold the balance of power between majorities which recognize their rights and majorities which deny them. Further, it is possible by decentralization to limit the power of the majority of the whole nation to questions upon which a divided policy is impracticable. . . .

In short, then, Democracy does not give majorities absolute power, nor does it enable them to reduce minorities to ciphers. Such limited power of coercing minorities as majorities must possess, is not given to them by Democracy any more than it can be taken away from them by Anarchism. A couple of men are stronger than one: that is all. There are only two ways of neutralizing this natural fact. One is to convince men of the immorality of abusing the majority power, and then to make them moral enough to refrain from doing it on that account.

The other is to realize Lytton's fancy of *vril* by inventing a means by which each individual will be able to destroy all his fellows with a flash of thought, so that the majority may have as much reason to fear the individual as he to fear the majority. No method of doing either is to be found in Individualist or Communist Anarchism: consequently these systems, as far as the evils of majority tyranny are concerned, are no better than the Social-Democratic program of adult suffrage with maintenance of representatives and payment of polling expenses from public funds—faulty devices enough, no doubt, but capable of accomplishing all that is humanly possible at present to make the State representative of the nation; to make the administration trustworthy; and to secure the utmost power to each individual and consequently to minorities. What better can we have whilst collective action is inevitable? Indeed, in the mouths of the really able Anarchists, Anarchism means simply the utmost attainable thoroughness of Democracy. Kropotkine, for example, speaks of free development from the simple to the composite by "the free union of free groups"; and his illustrations are "the societies for study, for commerce, for pleasure and recreation" which have sprung up to meet the varied requirements of the individual of our age. But in every one of these societies there is government by a council elected annually by a majority of voters; so that Kropotkine is not at all afraid of the democratic machinery and the majority power. Mr. Tucker speaks of "voluntary association," but gives no illustrations, and indeed avows that "Anarchists are simply unterrified Jeffersonian Democrats." He says, indeed, that "if the individual has a right to govern himself, all external government is tyranny"; but if governing oneself means doing what one pleases without regard to the interests of neighbors, then the individual has flatly no such right. If he has no such right, the interference of his neighbors to make him behave socially, though it is "external government," is not tyranny; and even if it were they would not refrain from it on that account. On the other hand, if governing oneself means compelling oneself to act with a due regard to the interests of the neighbors, then it is a right which men are proved incapable of exercizing without external government. Either way, the phrase comes to nothing; for it would be easy to show by little play upon it, either that altruism is really external government or that democratic State authority is really self-government.

Mr. Tucker's adjective, "voluntary," as applied to associations for defense or the management of affairs, must not be taken as implying that there is any very wide choice open in these matters. Such association is really compulsory, since if it be foregone affairs will remain unmanaged and communities defenseless. Nature makes short work of our aspirations toward utter impunity. She leaves communities in no wise "free" to choose whether they will labor and govern themselves. It is either that or starvation and chaos. Her tasks are inexorably set: her penalties are inevitable: her payment is strictly "payment by results." All the individual can do is to shift and dodge his share of the task on to the shoulders of others, or filch some of their "natural wage" to add to his own. If they are fools enough to suffer it, that is their own affair as far as Nature is concerned. But it is the aim of Social-Democracy to relieve these fools by throwing on all an equal share in the inevitable labor imposed by the eternal tyranny of Nature, and so secure to every individual no less than his equal quota of the nation's product in return for no more than his equal quota of the nation's labor. These are the best terms humanity can make with its tyrant. . . .

We can now begin to join the threads of our discussion. We have seen that private appropriation of land in any form, whether limited by Individualist Anarchism to occupying owners or not, means the unjust distribution of a vast fund of social wealth called rent, which can by no means be claimed as due to the labor of any particular individual or class of individuals. We have seen that Communist Anarchism, though it partly— and only partly—avoids the rent difficulty, is, in the condition of morals developed under existing Unsocialism, impracticable. We have seen that the delegation of individual powers by

voting; the creation of authoritative public bodies; the supremacy of the majority in the last resort; and the establishment
and even endowment, either directly and officially or indirectly
and unconsciously, of conventional forms of practice in religion, medicine, education, food, clothing, and criminal law,
are, whether they be evils or not, inherent in society itself, and
must be submitted to with the help of such protection against
their abuse as democratic institutions more than any others
afford. When Democracy fails, there is no antidote for intolerance save the spread of better sense. No form of Anarchism yet suggested provides any escape. Like bad weather in
winter, intolerance does much mischief; but as, when we have
done our best in the way of overcoats, umbrellas, and good
fires, we have to put up with the winter; so, when we have
done our best in the way of Democracy, decentralization and
the like, we must put up with the State.

I suppose I must not leave the subject without a word as to
the value of what I will call the Anarchist spirit as an element
in progress. . . . it must be understood that I do not stand here
to defend the State as we know it. Bakounine's comprehensive
aspiration to destroy all States and Established Churches, with
their religious, political, judicial, financial, criminal, academic,
economic, and social laws and institutions, seems to me perfectly justifiable and intelligible from the point of view of the
ordinary "educated man," who believes that institutions make
men instead of men making institutions. I fully admit and
vehemently urge that the State at present is simply a huge
machine for robbing and slave-driving the poor by brute force.
You may, if you are a stupid or comfortably-off person, think
that the policeman at the corner is the guardian of law and
order—that the gaol, with those instruments of torture, the
treadmill, plank bed, solitary cell, cat-o'-nine tails, and gal-
lows, is a place to make people cease to do evil and learn to do
well. But the primary function of the policeman, and that for
which his other functions are only blinds, is to see that you do not
lie down to sleep in this country without paying an idler for the
privilege; that you do not taste bread until you have paid the

idler's toll in the price of it; that you do not resist the starving blackleg who is dragging you down to his level for the idler's profit by offering to do your work for a starvation wage. Attempt any of these things, and you will be haled off and tortured in the name of law and order, honesty, social equilibrium, safety of property and person, public duty, Christianity, morality, and what not, as a vagrant, a thief, and a rioter. Your soldier, ostensibly a heroic and patriotic defender of his country, is really an unfortunate man driven by destitution to offer himself as food for powder for the sake of regular rations, shelter and clothing; and he must, on pain of being arbitrarily imprisoned, punished with petty penances like a naughty child, pack-drilled, flogged or shot, all in the blessed name of "discipline," do anything he is ordered to, from standing in his red coat in the hall of an opera house as a mere ornament, to flogging his comrade or committing murder. And *his* primary function is to come to the rescue of the policeman when the latter is overpowered. Members of Parliament whose sole qualifications for election were £1000 loose cash, an "independent" income, and a vulgar strain of ambition; parsons quoting scripture for the purposes of the squire; lawyers selling their services to the highest bidder at the bar, and maintaining the supremacy of the moneyed class on the bench; juries of employers masquerading as the peers of proletarians in the dock; University professors elaborating the process known as the education of a gentleman; artists striving to tickle the fancy or flatter the vanity of the aristocrat or plutocrat; workmen doing their work as badly and slowly as they dare so as to make the most of their job; employers starving and overworking their hands and adulterating their goods as much as *they* dare: these are the actual living material of those imposing abstractions known as the State, the Church, the Law, the Constitution, Education, the Fine Arts, and Industry. Every institution, as Bakounine saw, religious, political, financial, judicial, and so on, is corrupted by the fact that the men in it either belong to the propertied class themselves or must sell themselves to it in order to live. All the purchasing power that is left to buy men's souls with after their bodies are fed is in the hands of the rich; and everywhere, from the Parliament which wields the irresistible coercive forces of the bludgeon, bayonet, machine gun, dynamite shell, prison and scaffold, down to the pettiest center of shabby-genteel social pretension, the rich pay the piper and call the tune. Naturally, they use their power to steal more money to continue paying the piper; and thus all society becomes a huge conspiracy and hypocrisy. The ordinary man is insensible to the fraud just as he is insensible to the taste of water, which, being constantly in contact with his mucous membrane, seems to have no taste at all. The villainous moral conditions on which our social system is based are necessarily in constant contact with our moral mucous membrane, and so we lose our sense of their omnipresent meanness and dishonor. The insensibility, however, is not quite complete; for there is a period in life which is called the age of disillusion, which means the age at which a man discovers that his generous and honest impulses are incompatible with success in business; that the institutions he has reverenced are shams; and that he must join the conspiracy or go to the wall, even though he feels that the conspiracy is fundamentally ruinous to himself and his fellow-conspirators. The secret of writers like Ruskin, Morris, and Kropotkine is that they see the whole imposture through and through, in spite of its familiarity, and of the illusions created by its temporal power, its riches, its spendor, its prestige, its intense respectability, its unremitting piety, and its high moral pretension.

. . . the Social-Democrat is compelled, by contact with hard facts, to turn his back decisively on useless denunciation of the State. It is easy to say, Abolish the State; but the State will sell you up, lock you up, blow you up, knock you down, bludgeon, shoot, stab, hang—in short, abolish you, if you lift a hand against it. Fortunately, there is, as we have seen, a fine impartiality about the policeman and the soldier, who are the cutting edge of the State power. They take their wages and obey their orders without asking questions. If those orders are to demolish the homestead of every peasant who refuses to take the bread out of his children's mouths in order that his landlord may have money to spend as an idle gentleman in London, the soldier obeys. But if his orders were to help the police to pitch his lordship into Holloway Gaol until he had paid an Income Tax of twenty shillings on every pound of his unearned income, the soldier would do that with equal devotion to duty, and perhaps with a certain private zest that might be lacking in the other case. Now these orders come ultimately from the State—meaning, in this country, the House of Commons. A House of Commons consisting of 660 gentlemen and 10 workmen will order the soldier to take money from the people for the landlords. A House of Commons consisting of 660 workmen and 10 gentlemen will probably, unless the 660 are fools, order the soldier to take money from the landlords for the people. With that hint I leave the matter, in the full conviction that the State, in spite of the Anarchists, will continue to be used against the people by the classes until it is used by the people against the classes with equal ability and equal resolution.

9 The Philosophical Anarchist

WILLIAM ERNEST HOCKING

William Ernest Hocking (1873–1966) was one of the most distinguished and admired of American philosophers. Long a professor of philosophy at Harvard University, he wrote extensively in many different philosophical fields. While he had no systematic philosophical position of his own, he drew upon both idealism and pragmatism, combining them into what sometimes was called "objective idealism." His viewpoint here is that of a moral philosopher, with a political outlook which is neutral by comparison with most writers on anarchism.

I say there can be no salvation for These States without innovators—without free tongues, and ears willing to hear
the tongues;
And I announce as a glory of These States, that they respect-
fully listen to propositions, reforms, fresh views and
doctrines.

WALT WHITMAN, *Leaves of Grass,* Says, 3.

The voluntary groupings of men have life in them; some of them have capacity and intelligence enough, the pluralist tells us, to bend, or control, or defy the policy of the government. But if this is so, why may they not, either now or later, wholly take its place? Why may we not look forward to a society of free, naturally interlacing, self-governing private groups? This is the question put by the philosophical anarchist.

From *Man and the State* (New Haven: Yale University Press, 1926), pp. 90–103. Copyright © 1926 by Yale University Press. Hocking's notes and section numbers have been omitted.

Note that if anarchy is equivalent to chaos, the philosophical anarchist, despite his name, is no seeker of anarchy. He calls for an end not of law but of laws and of law-enforcement. Nor does he advise that government should be at once done away, ending its force by violence. His plan (if we may make a type of schemes so various) is that the activities of government shall be diminished by degrees until, when only the administering of public services is left, private associations may take them over.

In its opposition to force, anarchism is akin to the belief that war between states can be and ought to be banished: anarchism is pacifism in internal affairs. In its opposition to governmental activity, it is akin to an ideal widely professed during the last century under the name of *laissez faire*, and still of popular vogue in the belief that "the state governs best that governs least." Most Americans are instinctive laissez-faireists in the respect that they dislike being reminded of government, believing in their capacity and that of their neighbors to manage their own affairs and their mutual affairs on terms of fair play without the surveillance of public authorities; and most incline subconsciously to philosophical anarchism, in so far as they assume, with Spinoza, that if man were completely socialized in his nature, as some day he may be, there would be no need for the state. Laissez-faireists differ from anarchists not so much in their ideal as in their view of the possibilities of human nature. The former think that the self-seeking and deceitful elements of human nature will remain statistically about as they are, requiring the police functions as an irreducible minimum of state activity; the latter believe in a moral progress such that the social casing of coercion may eventually be discarded, leaving a matured, self-respecting humanity to maintain freely its order and character. They believe, further, that the gradual decrease of state pressure would hasten this event, because human nature has a bent to goodness, and gives the best account of itself when unfettered by artificial requirements.

As for the criminal, his existence is not forgotten; but it is thought that he is either such by definition only, as one who has disobeyed what *we* have commanded; or he is such by response to the unnatural environment of the state and the exaggerated inequalities which it fosters; or else he is the unusual individual of determined ill-will who is best dealt with by near and private hands, since the life of the will, whether for good or for evil, is always intimate, individual, and unique. The legal separation between sheep and goats is too obviously an affair of exteriors to satisfy the anarchist's thirst for inner realities.

He is not disposed to minimize the need of settling disputes, as a condition of keeping social groups alive. He is not less but rather more impressed than most men with the necessity as well as the beauty of reasonableness, self-control, and cumulative understandings among men. His difference from those who hold to the state is simply that he believes that these goods should be and can be supplied by men themselves, not imposed upon them by an external power.

This faith of the anarchist in the capacity of human nature for association at once forceless and orderly is not wholly *a priori*. In the nature of the case, modern experiments in anarchism have been confined to small communities living within and under the general law of existing states. Still, communities have existed which were nearly devoid of organized public force, except such as formed itself spontaneously as occasion demanded. The early Jewish community was of this character. In its case, a tenacious religious faith made possible a direction of public affairs uniquely informal and noncoercive. And while that faith cannot be reproduced, a moral equivalent is conceivable.

But the chief evidence is nearer at hand, in the same facts as lead the more cautious thinker to pluralism, namely, the abundant vital energy of voluntary groups, their natural authority, and growing capacity for self-government. Consider, for example, the immense growth in recent years of cooperative associations of producers, consumers, builders, etc., including now some thirty millions of members in Europe and America; and remember that such groups can succeed only as they impose upon themselves the rigorous discipline required for economic stability. Consider also how the development of codes of business practice, and the extension of the art of voluntary agreement on business standards, is beginning to take the place of legislation and to relieve the burdens of the courts.

Continued neighborhood and a common economy have been from time immemorial the great teachers of natural order to mankind. To this day, vast agricultural regions carry on a custom-controlled life, hardly aware of the existence of the state except as tax-gatherer and conscriptionist. Agriculture is also man-culture; all normal growth is from the soil upward. It is an empirical growth, based on experience well-mastered, and therefore sound and enduring.

Quite apart, then, from the moral force which the anarchist may feel in himself and attribute to human nature at large, there is ground for his faith in the possibilities of an ultimately free community. But he is moved to this alternative, whose difficulty he does not conceal from himself, chiefly by a poignant sense of the evils to which all social control, and especially all force-using government, is subject.

The most concrete of these evils, to the traditional anarchist, is the enforcement of economic inequity. The economy built up from the immediate contact of individual men with soil and region and neighbor is sound, because, as we have said, it is empirical. The state is associated with an artificial economy, *brought to* labor and the soil from outside, an economy ordered about a protected mass of capital, perpetuating itself by inheritance, claiming the primacy and eternity of the general idea, a practical *a priori*. Anarchism is hostile to this inherited privilege, this self-perpetuating and cumulative mass, which it finds represented to the workers chiefly in the toll which it takes from them to support its own life, in Proudhon's view a fundamental theft.

But while the existence of capital as a social acquisition may create the motive for a capitalistic state, it is not intrinsic to the idea of the state that it should enforce capitalism or any other economic order. And hostility to capitalism is, of course, not peculiar to anarchism. The evils to which the anarchist is peculiarly sensitive lie deeper, in the very nature of a coercive society.

Social belonging is in no case an unmixed good. Every group exerts a pressure upon its members which tends to standardize them and warp them from their own true. Assuming as it must that many individuals are alike in that portion of their lives which it lives for them, the group blankets and obscures individual differences of will and power. When the state is described as "an external form given to the moral will," it might seem that government is being given a good character. But is it unquestionably good to belong to a group which assumes to do for me (even if it does it well) part of the work of my own conscience,—after all, an inalienable organ. If it is indeed my own will which comes back to me through the state, why must I be compelled to accept my own as the voice of another and to live so far a vicarious life? Why must I be placed in the peril of not recognizing my own conscience in what is required of me? The inescapable pressure of the majority upon the minority, more particularly upon that omnipresent minority of *one* constituted by each one's individual judgment, becomes most intolerable when it is the moral judgment that is involved.

The effect of belonging upon character is clearly perceptible. In the wilds one feels more directly the natural man. If he is weak, the state lends him no adventitious strength: the "rights" which he has in common with every other citizen he must stand up for, if they are to count in his favor. His neighbors will not restrain themselves on behalf of a specter of unmanned legality: they restrain themselves in the presence of the man they personally respect. Thus the native forces of character must make themselves felt, and they thrive under the necessity. On the other hand, where the political environment is compact, and every moral weakling may count himself safe from violence and fraud, men of large powers may find themselves ill at ease: too much is done and willed for them—their qualities fail to tell. They may find themselves deficient in that special knack of self-alienation which enables lesser men to take firm root in the settled order. To rely on the police and the law court for protection and justice brings with it a subtle sense of shame and undue dependence.

Capacity to accept this vicarious moral living and this sharing of self-help is regarded as a part of civic virtue. Yet, other things equal, how can such renunciation of personal completeness be other than a diminishing of manhood? Unless there is an energy of personal growth great enough to carry its self-assertion into new fields, while leaving the socially shared self in the region of habit, the political man is surely in some ways less noble than the semi-anarchic pioneer.

The same "if" must be written against all social belonging. It offers at once a possibility and a danger—a possibility of growing in some directions beyond any dream of solitude, a danger of falling below the natural level by a morally parasitic and passively conforming relation to the social mentality. But in the case of the state these dangers are magnified by the element of coercion; and as the anarchist sees them, they develop into specific evils inseparable from life under government.

First of them is the *restriction of liberty*; and liberty, in the anarchist's ideal, is the chief of all political goods. If liberty is the chief political good, then no sacrifice of it for any other good can be other than a bad bargain.

Society stands to lose by every diminution of general freedom; for it runs the risk of checking its most original, and therefore most priceless, developments. Though not every divergent genius is a prophet, the prophets are bound to be among the divergent and intractable. Yet it is not in the name of the social welfare that the anarchist primarily pleads his cause. It is in the name of the individual's own destiny and right.

Life itself is individual, and the most significant things in the world—perhaps in the end the only significant things—are individual souls. Each one of these must work its own way to salvation, win its own experience, suffer from its own mistakes: "through angers, losses, ambition, ignorance, ennui," yes, and through crime and retribution, "what you are picks its way." Any rule which by running human conduct into approved grooves saves men from this salutary Odyssey thwarts the first meaning of human life.

In the second place, so far as the state requires good of men it *deprives that good of moral value.* For only that can have moral value which comes from free choice. Whatever is required by law is therefore drained of moral quality.

The actual ethical condition of the best governed states seems to confirm this criticism. Who does not recognize that in the typical political civilization of today conformity has largely replaced conscience, outer respectability takes the place of an inoperative personal conviction about conduct, and the fiber of men decays. Absence of moral originality is not the normal state of mankind: it is only in urbane communities that "what is done" becomes the complete guide to the practice of ruler and ruled alike.

Finally, there is the long history of the *abuse* of power. The unholy accompaniments of coercion, in "free" states as well as in others, the subtle poison of possessing force, the moral perdition in assuming the right to judge and punish, the blearing of the official eye to all that is individual through the pressure of business and the mechanism of the general rule, the callousness and the shifting of responsibility bred of the belief in the efficiency of the machine and the sufficiency of what has been—these are evils which are no specialties of cruel and cruder eras of mankind: they are the predictable incidents of bringing weak humanity into the false position of control over its fellows.

And the result is that enforced law shares the fate of all abnormalities—it *undermines its own position.*

For however worthy of obedience the law may be, governments, seduced by force-using, seldom are; and the disaffection from rulers extends to the law behind them. There is an element of arrogance in their wielding of principles more sacred than themselves; and if they insist on being inseparable from the law, the resentment due them will not be withheld because it strikes the law also. Law which allies itself with force begets lawlessness.

Those who justify themselves in evading the Volstead Act on

the ground that it is foisted upon an unwilling majority by a group of determined bigots are not different in this respect from most other lawbreakers. They scent a personal factor in the law which is repellent to them; they extend this repulsion to the law, to its enforcers, and thus to the fabric of government. The anarchist argues that this is a psychological result which must appear in all men subject to government: sooner or later spontaneous lawfulness is destroyed.

In sum, the ultimate animus of anarchism is a deep sense of the crime which an enforced organization inflicts upon life, which is by birthright free, individual, varied.

Organization is in its nature impersonal; it can deal only in the common denominators of personality, the abstract elements of will. If it touches men powerfully, it invites them to accept its generalized human being in place of their concrete selfhood, and thus dehumanizes those with whom it converses.

In this impersonality, the moral quality is diluted and tends to disappear in the statistics of a mythical general welfare. The human friend and the human opponent have vanished into general tendencies; and in the name of their states men fight enemies whom no one hates, supporting friends whom no one loves, committing crimes which burden no one's conscience because they seem to fall in the world of the ghostly political entities, not in the world of human life. England may force opium on China when no Englishman would force opium on any human individual. Nationality thus becomes, in the impassioned words of Tagore, "one of the most powerful anaesthetics that man has invented."

And all organization tends to propagate itself, as men analyze out of their own being more and more of the common elements. The logic of combined power carries an irresistible argument, once you submit yourself to it: power must be met by power; neither the state nor any part of it can submit to be overrun, and men must sell all, as Hobbes would have them do, to be strong. But this logic of power, shrewdly regarding every neighbor as the potential enemy, is incompatible with the growth of the human quality. At last you must choose between it and the development of the soul or the achievement of a humane society.

So far, the anarchistic point of view, the necessary background of all political philosophy.

To estimate the argument of the anarchist, we must begin by recognizing that the evils he mentions exist, and the psychological tendencies that give rise to them. Our question must be whether these evils are inseparable from government; and if so, whether the value of government is so great as to outweigh them.

It cannot be denied, I think, that law has some tendency to breed lawlessness. Certainly, law-enforcement always has a back-stroke to reckon with. There is something in every human temper (and more in some than in others) which replies to a command with a retort, "Remove the compulsion, and I will do freely what you wish."

But this element of balk diminishes as the command becomes a general regulation, and therefore not personally directed. In the course of nature, human beings arrive at self-government by way of a long regime of parental coercion. The presence of coercion, therefore, cannot be incompatible with the growth of spontaneous lawfulness. Moral self-control does find its way somehow beneath the cover of external constraint. And when family discipline gives way to the relative "freedom" of maturity, what is this freedom except life under the coercive state? Evidently this coercion does not largely cross the path of ordinary self-management. Governments could hardly exist unless the great majority of citizens, with respect to the great bulk of the law, were law-abiding without knowing it and therefore without resenting it. The punishment of murder by death may incite some few to buy guns; it may deter some who otherwise would buy them; but to most of us, to gun or not to gun has simply ceased to be a live issue. Except in the case of laws which encroach upon the province of customary self-control and so have a peculiarly irritating implication, like the Volstead Act, we may dismiss the tendency of the fact of government to breed lawlessness as an actual but minor factor in the political life of today, whereas the alleged incompatibility between compulsion and moral initiative is a plain psychological error.

As to the restriction of liberty, the anarchist's contention is not so easily disposed of. We may remark that in any group the restraint upon freedom is proportionate to the area of contact between members. It is greatest, therefore, in the most intimate associations, as the family, least in the least intimate. Those who, like Mr. Bertrand Russell, call for a type of marriage in which neither partner breathes upon the liberty of the other, call in effect for the abolition of marriage. Restraint in the state will be, in the nature of the case, far less pervasive than in the family; but the issues, when the wills of state and citizens clash, will be none the less keen for that, and may be as momentous for the citizen.

But it is evident the questions which the anarchist raises are questions of human nature. He invites us to think of its possibilities in one respect more highly and in another respect less highly than we are accustomed. More highly in respect to the capacity of large masses of the governed for good will and eventual self-control. Less highly in respect to the capacity of governors to resist the seductions of power. In advance, one might suppose that since governors, in most modern states, are bred from the same stock with the governed, the perfectibility of the governed would bring that of the governors with it, and lessen the power of organization to corrupt the spiritual principle in both.

But we cannot give a final answer to anarchism until we have met for ourselves the psychological questions it raises—questions of the capacity and moral future of human nature. Meanwhile, both pluralism and anarchism press for an answer to the question: What is it that so distinguishes the state from other groups as to lend color to its pretense to ascendency? What is that unique purpose of the state which contains the secret of its claim to use force?

10 Government and Law

BERTRAND RUSSELL

Bertrand Russell (1872-1970) was one of the greatest philosophers and mathematicians of this century; he won the Nobel Prize for Literature in 1950. Long dedicated to unpopular causes and extremely active in their advocacy, he was often a center of violent controversy throughout his long life. This critique of anarchism was written from a moderate socialist perspective.

Government and Law, in their very essence, consist of restrictions on freedom, and freedom is the greatest of political goods. A hasty reasoner might conclude without further ado that Law and government are evils which must be abolished if freedom is our goal. But this consequence, true or false, cannot be proved so simply. We shall examine the arguments of Anarchists against law and the State. We shall proceed on the assumption that freedom is the supreme aim of a good social system; but on this very basis we shall find the Anarchist contentions very questionable.

Respect for the liberty of others is not a natural impulse with most men: envy and love of power lead ordinary human

From *Proposed Roads to Freedom* (London: George Allen & Unwin, 1919 and 1966, and New York: Barnes & Nobel, 1966), pp. 111–34, 136–38. Reprinted by permission of the copyright holders, George Allen & Unwin and Barnes & Noble. The text is here somewhat condensed.

nature to find pleasure in interferences with the lives of others. If all men's actions were wholly unchecked by external authority, we should not obtain a world in which all men would be free. The strong would oppress the weak, or the majority would oppress the minority, or the lovers of violence would oppress the more peaceable people. I fear it cannot be said that these bad impulses are *wholly* due to a bad social system, though it must be conceded that the present competitive organization of society does a great deal to foster the worst elements in human nature. The love of power is an impulse which, though innate in very ambitious men, is chiefly promoted as a rule by the actual experience of power. In a world where none could acquire much power, the desire to tyrannize would be much less strong than it is at present. Nevertheless, I cannot think that it would be wholly absent, and those in whom it would exist would often be men of unusual energy and executive capacity. Such men, if they are not restrained by the organized will of the community, may either succeed in establishing a despotism, or, at any rate, make such a vigorous attempt as can only be defeated through a period of prolonged disturbance. And apart from the love or political power, there is the love of power over individuals. If threats and terrorism were not prevented by law, it can hardly be doubted that cruelty would be rife in the relations of men and women, and of parents and children. It is true that the habits of a community can make such cruelty rare, but these habits, I fear, are only to be produced through the prolonged reign of law. Experience of backwoods communities, mining camps and other such places seems to show that under new conditions men easily revert to a more barbarous attitude and practice. It would seem, therefore, that, while human nature remains as it is, there will be more liberty for all in a community where some acts of tyranny by individuals are forbidden, than in a community where the law leaves each individual free to follow his every impulse. But, although the necessity of some form of government and law must for the present be conceded, it is important to remember that all law and government is in itself in some degree an evil, only justifiable when it prevents other and greater evils. Every use of the power of the State needs, therefore, to be very closely scrutinized, and every possibility of diminishing its power is to be welcomed provided it does not lead to a reign of private tyranny.

The power of the State is partly legal, partly economic: acts of a kind which the state dislikes can be punished by the criminal law, and individuals who incur the displeasure of the State may find it hard to earn a livelihood.

The views of Marx on the State are not very clear. On the one hand he seems willing, like the modern State Socialists, to allow great power to the State, but on the other hand he suggests that when the Socialist revolution has been consummated, the State, as we know it, will disappear. Among the measures which are advocated in the Communist Manifesto as immediately desirable, there are several which would very greatly increase the power of the existing State. For example, "Centralization of credit in the hands of the State, by means of a national bank with State capital and an exclusive monopoly"; and again, "Centralization of the means of communication and transport in the hands of the State." But the Manifesto goes on to say:

> When, in the course of development, class distinctions have disappeared, and all production has been concentrated in the hands of a vast association of the whole nation, the public power will lose its political character. Political power, properly so called, is merely the organised power of one class for oppressing another. If the proletariat during its contest with the bourgéoisie is compelled, by the force of circumstances, to organize itself as a class, if, by means of a revolution, it makes itself the ruling class, and, as such, sweeps away by force the old conditions of production, then it will, along with these conditions, have swept away the conditions for the existence of class antagonisms, and of classes generally, and will thereby have abolished its own supremacy as a class.
>
> In place of the old bourgeois society, with its classes and class antagonisms, we shall have an association, in which the free development of each is the condition for the free development of all. . . .

Among all these different views, the one which raises the deepest issue is the Anarchist contention that all coercion by the community is unnecessary. Like most of the things that Anarchists say, there is much more to be urged in support of this view than most people would suppose at first sight. Kropotkin, who is its ablest exponent, points out how much has been achieved already by the method of free agreement. He does not wish to abolish government in the sense of collective decisions: what he does wish to abolish is the system by which a decision is enforced upon those who oppose it. The whole system of representative government and majority rule is to him a bad thing. He points to such instances as the agreements among the different railway systems of the Continent for the running of through expresses and for cooperation generally. He points out that in such cases the different companies or authorities concerned each appoint a delegate, and that the delegates suggest a basis of agreement, which has to be subsequently ratified by each of the bodies appointing them. The assembly of delegates has no coercive power whatever, and a majority can do nothing against a recalcitrant minority. Yet this has not prevented the conclusion of very elaborate systems of agreements. By such methods, so Anarchists contend, the *useful* functions of government can be carried out without any coercion. They maintain that the usefulness of agreement is so patent as to make cooperation certain if once the predatory motives associated with the present system of private property were removed.

Attractive as this view is, I cannot resist the conclusion that it results from impatience and represents the attempt to find a short-cut toward the ideal which all humane people desire.

Let us begin with the question of private crime. Anarchists maintain that the criminal is manufactured by bad social conditions and would disappear in such a world as they aim at creating. No doubt there is a great measure of truth in this view. There would be little motive to robbery, for example, in an Anarchist world, unless it were organized on a large scale by a body of men bent on upsetting the Anarchist *régime*. It may also be conceded that impulses toward criminal violence could be very largely eliminated by a better education. But all such contentions, it seems to me, have their limitations. To take an extreme case, we cannot suppose that there would be no lunatics in an Anarchist community, and some of these lunatics would, no doubt, be homicidal. Probably no one would argue that they ought to be left at liberty. But there are no sharp lines in nature; from the homicidal lunatic to the sane man of violent passions there is a continuous gradation. Even in the most perfect community there will be men and women, otherwise sane, who will feel an impulse to commit murder from jealousy. These are now usually restrained by the fear of punishment, but if this fear were removed, such murders would probably become much more common, as may be seen from the present behavior of certain soldiers on leave. Moreover, certain kinds of conduct arouse public hostility, and would almost inevitably lead to lynching, if no other recognized method of punishment existed. There is in most men a certain natural vindictiveness, not always directed against the worst members of the community. For example, Spinoza was very nearly murdered by the mob because he was suspected of undue friendliness to France at a time when Holland was at war with that country. Apart from such cases, there would be the very real danger of an organized attempt to destroy Anarchism and revive ancient oppressions. Is it to be supposed, for example, that Napoleon, if he had been born into such a community as Kropotkin advocates, would have acquiesced tamely in a world where his genius could find no scope? I cannot see what should prevent a combination of ambitious men forming themselves into a private army, manufacturing their own munitions, and at last enslaving the defenseless citizens, who had relied upon the inherent attractiveness of liberty. It would not be consistent with the principles of Anarchism for the community to interfere with the drilling of a private army, no matter what its object might be (though, of course, an opposing private army might be formed by men with different views). Indeed, Kropotkin instances the old volunteers in Great Britain as an example of a movement on Anarchist lines. Even if a predatory army were not formed from within, it might easily come from a neighboring nation, or from races on the borderland of civilization. So long as the love of power exists, I do not see how it can be prevented from finding an outlet in oppression except by means of the organized force of the community.

The conclusion, which appears to be forced upon us, is that the Anarchist ideal of a community in which no acts are forbidden by law is not, at any rate for the present, compatible with the stability of such a world as the Anarchists desire. In order to obtain and preserve a world resembling as closely as possible that at which they aim, it will still be necessary that some acts should be forbidden by law. We may put the chief of these under three heads: (1) Theft; (2) Crimes of violence; (3) The creation of organizations intended to subvert the Anarchist *régime* by force. We will briefly recapitulate what has been said already as to the necessity of these prohibitions.

Theft. It is true that in an Anarchist world there will be no destitution, and therefore no thefts motivated by starvation. But such thefts are at present by no means the most considerable or the most harmful. The system of rationing, which is to be applied to luxuries, will leave many men with fewer luxuries than they might desire. It will give opportunities for peculation by those who are in control of the public stores, and it will leave the possibility of appropriating such valuable objects of art as would naturally be preserved in public museums. It may be contended that such forms of theft would be prevented by public opinion. But public opinion is not greatly operative upon an individual unless it is the opinion of his own group. A group of men combined for purposes of theft might readily defy the public opinion of the majority unless that public opinion made itself effective by the use of force against them. Probably, in fact, such force would be applied through popular indignation, but in that case we should revive the evils of the criminal law with the added evils of uncertainty, haste and passion, which are inseparable from the practice of lynching. If, as we have suggested, it were found necessary to provide an economic stimulus to work by allowing fewer luxuries to idlers, this would afford a new motive for theft on their part and a new necessity for some form of criminal law.

Crimes of Violence. Cruelty to children, crimes of jealousy, rape, and so forth, are almost certain to occur in any society to some extent. The prevention of such acts is essential to the existence of freedom for the weak. If nothing were done to hinder them, it is to be feared that the customs of a society would gradually become rougher, and that acts which are now rare would cease to be so. If Anarchists are right in maintaining that the existence of such an economic system as they desire would prevent the commission of crimes of this kind, the laws forbidding them would no longer come into operation, and would do no harm to liberty. If, on the other hand, the impulse to such actions persisted, it would be necessary that steps should be taken to restrain men from indulging it.

The third class of difficulties is much the most serious and involves much the most drastic interference with liberty. I do not see how a private army could be tolerated within an Anarchist community, and I do not see how it could be prevented except by a general prohibition of carrying arms. If there were no such prohibition, rival parties would organize rival forces, and civil war would result. Yet, if there is such a prohibition, it cannot well be carried out without a very considerable interference with individual liberty. No doubt, after a time, the idea of using violence to achieve a political object might die down, as the practice of dueling has done. But such changes of habit and outlook are facilitated by legal prohibition, and would hardly come about without it. I shall not speak yet of the international aspect of this same problem, but it is clear that the same considerations apply with even greater force to the relations between nations.

If we admit, however reluctantly, that a criminal law is necessary and that the force of the community must be brought to bear to prevent certain kinds of actions, a further question arises: How is crime to be treated? What is the greatest measure of humanity and respect for freedom that is compatible with the recognition of such a thing as crime? The first thing to recognize is that the whole conception of guilt or sin should be utterly swept away. At present, the criminal is visited with the displeasure of the community: the sole method applied to prevent the occurrence of crime is the infliction of pain upon the criminal. Everything possible is done to break his spirit and destroy his self-respect. Even those pleasures which would be most likely to have a civilizing effect are forbidden to him, merely on the ground that they are pleasures, while much of the suffering inflicted is of a kind which can only brutalize and degrade still further. I am not speaking, of course, of those few penal institutions which have made a serious study of reforming the criminal. Such institutions, especially in America, have been proved capable of achieving the most remarkable results, but they remain everywhere exceptional. The broad rule is still that the criminal is made to feel the displeasure of society. He must emerge from such a treatment either defiant and hostile, or submissive and cringing, with a broken spirit and a loss of self-respect. Neither of these results is anything but evil. Nor can any good result be achieved by a method of treatment which embodies reprobation.

When a man is suffering from an infectious disease he is a danger to the community, and it is necessary to restrict his liberty of movement. But no one associates any idea of guilt with such a situation. On the contrary, he is an object of commiseration to his friends. Such steps as science recommends are taken to cure him of his disease, and he submits as a rule without reluctance to the curtailment of liberty involved meanwhile. The same method in spirit ought to be shown in the treatment of what is called "crime." It is supposed, of course, that the criminal is actuated by calculations of self-interest, and that the fear of punishment, by supplying a contrary motive of self-interest affords the best deterrent.

> The dog, to gain some private end,
> Went mad and bit the man.

This is the popular view of crime; yet no dog goes mad from choice, and probably the same is true of the great majority of criminals, certainly in the case of crimes of passion. Even in cases where self-interest is the motive, the important thing is to prevent the crime, not to make the criminal suffer. Any suffering which may be entailed by the process of prevention ought to be regarded as regrettable, like the pain involved in a surgical operation. The man who commits a crime from an impulse to violence ought to be subjected to a scientific psychological treatment, designed to elicit more beneficial impulses. The man who commits a crime from calculations of self-interest ought to be made to feel that self-interest itself, when it is fully understood, can be better served by a life which is useful to the community than by one which is harmful. For this purpose it is chiefly necessary to widen his outlook and increase the scope of his desires. At present, when a man suffers from insufficient love for his fellow-creatures, the method of curing him which is commonly adopted seems scarcely designed to succeed, being, indeed, in essentials, the same as his attitude toward them. The object of the prison administration is to save trouble, not to study the individual case. He is kept in captivity in a cell from which all sight of the earth is shut out: he is subjected to harshness by warders, who have too often become brutalized by their occupation. He is solemnly denounced as an enemy to society. He is compelled to perform mechanical tasks, chosen for their wearisomeness. He is given no education and no incentive to self-improvement. Is it to be wondered at if, at the end of such a course of treatment, his feelings toward the community are no more friendly than they were at the beginning?

Severity of punishment arose through vindictiveness and fear in an age when many criminals escaped justice altogether, and it was hoped that savage sentences would outweigh the chance of escape in the mind of the criminal. At present a very large part of the criminal law is concerned in safeguarding the rights of property, that is to say—as things are now—the unjust privileges of the rich. Those whose principles lead them into conflict with government, like Anarchists, bring a most formidable indictment against the law and the authorities for the unjust manner in which they support the *status quo*. Many of the actions by which men have become rich are far more harmful to the community than the obscure crimes of poor men, yet they go unpunished because they do not interfere with the existing order. If the power of the community is to be brought to bear to prevent certain classes of actions through the agency of the criminal law, it is as necessary that these actions should really be those which are harmful to the community, as it is that the treatment of "criminals" should be freed from the conception of guilt and inspired by the same spirit as is shown in the treatment of disease. But, if these two conditions were fulfilled, I cannot help thinking that a society which preserved the existence of law would be preferable to one conducted on the unadulterated principles of Anarchism.

So far we have been considering the power which the State derives from the criminal law. We have every reason to think that this power cannot be entirely abolished, though it can be exercised in a wholly different spirit, without the vindictiveness and the moral reprobation which now form its essence.

We come next to the consideration of the economic power of the State and the influence which it can exert through its bureaucracy. State Socialists argue as if there would be no danger to liberty in a State not based upon capitalism. This seems to me an entire delusion. Given an official caste, however selected, there are bound to be a set of men whose whole instincts will drive them toward tyranny. Together with the natural love of power, they will have a rooted conviction (visible now in the higher ranks of the Civil Service) that they alone know enough to be able to judge what is for the good of the community. Like all men who administer a system, they will come to feel the system itself sacrosanct. The only changes they will desire will be changes in the direction of further regulations as to how the people are to enjoy the good things kindly granted to them by their benevolent despots. Whoever thinks this picture overdrawn must have failed to study the influence and methods of Civil Servants at present. On every matter that arises, they know far more than the general public about all the *definite* facts involved; the one thing they do not know is "where the shoe pinches." But those who know this are probably not skilled in stating their case, not able to say off-hand exactly how many shoes are pinching how many feet, or what is the precise remedy required. The answer prepared for Ministers by the Civil Service is accepted by the "respectable" public as impartial, and is regarded as disposing of the case of malcontents except on a first-class political question on which elections may be won or lost. That at least is the way in which things are managed in England. And there is every reason to fear that under State Socialism the power of officials would be vastly greater than it is at present.

Those who accept the orthodox doctrine of democracy contend that, if ever the power of capital were removed, representative institutions would suffice to undo the evils threatened by bureaucracy. Against this view, Anarchists and Syndicalists have directed a merciless criticism. French Syndicalists especially, living, as they do, in a highly democratized country, have had bitter experience of the way in which the power of the State can be employed against a progressive minority. This experience has led them to abandon altogether the belief in the divine right of majorities. The Constitution that they would desire would be one which allowed scope for vigorous minorities, conscious of their aims and prepared to work for them. It is undeniable that, to all who care for progress, actual experience of democratic representative Government is very disillusioning. Admitting—as I think we must—that it is preferable to any *previous* form of Government, we must yet acknowledge that much of the criticism directed against it by Anarchists and Syndicalists is thoroughly justified.

Such criticism would have had more influence if any clear idea of an alternative to parliamentary democracy had been generally apprehended. But it must be confessed that Syndicalists have not presented their case in a way which is likely to attract the average citizen. Much of what they say amounts to this: that a minority, consisting of skilled workers in vital industries, can, by a strike, make the economic life of the whole community impossible, and can in this way force their will upon the nation. The action aimed at is compared to the seizure of a power station, by which a whole vast system can be paralyzed. Such a doctrine is an appeal to force, and is naturally met by an appeal to force on the other side. It is useless for the Syndicalists to protest that they only desire power in order to promote liberty: the world which they are seeking to establish does not, as yet, appeal to the effective will of the community, and cannot be stably inaugurated until it does do so. Persuasion is a slow process, and may sometimes be accelerated by violent methods; to this extent such methods may be justified. But the ultimate goal of any reformer who aims at liberty can only be reached through persuasion. The attempt to thrust liberty by force upon those who do not desire what we consider liberty must always prove a failure; and Syndicalists, like other reformers, must ultimately rely upon persuasion for success.

But it would be a mistake to confuse aims with methods: however little we may agree with the proposal to force the millennium on a reluctant community by starvation, we may yet agree that much of what the Syndicalists desire to achieve is desirable.

Let us dismiss from our minds such criticisms of parliamentary government as are bound up with the present system of private property, and consider only those which would remain true in a collectivist community. Certain defects seem inherent in the very nature of representative institutions. There is a sense of self-importance, inseparable from success in a contest for popular favor. There is an all-but unavoidable habit of hypocrisy, since experience shows that the democracy does not detect insincerity in an orator, and will, on the other hand, be shocked by things which even the most sincere men may think necessary. Hence arises a tone of cynicism among elected representatives, and a feeling that no man can retain his position in politics without deceit. This is as much the fault of the democracy as of the representatives, but it seems unavoidable so long as the main thing that all bodies of men demand of their champions is flattery. However the blame may be apportioned, the evil must be recognized as one which is bound to occur in the existing forms of democracy. Another evil, which is especially noticeable in large States, is the remoteness of the seat of government from many of the constituencies—a remoteness which is psychological even more than geographical. The legislators live in comfort, protected by thick walls and innumerable policemen from the voice of the mob; as time goes on they remember only dimly the passions and promises of their electoral campaign; they come to feel it an essential part of statesmanship to consider what are called the interests of the community as a whole, rather than those of some discontented group; but the interests of the community as a whole are sufficiently vague to be easily seen to coincide with self-interest. All these causes lead Parliaments to betray the people, consciously or unconsciously; and it is no wonder if they have produced a certain aloofness from democratic theory in the more vigorous champions of labor.

Majority rule, as it exists in large States, is subject to the fatal defect that, in a very great number of questions, only a fraction of the nation have any direct interest or knowledge, yet the others have an equal voice in their settlement. When people have no direct interest in a question they are very apt to be influenced by irrelevant considerations; this is shown in the extraordinary reluctance to grant autonomy to subordinate nations or groups. For this reason, it is very dangerous to allow the nation as a whole to decide on matters which concern only a small section, whether that section be geographical or industrial or defined in any other way. The best cure for this evil, so far as can be seen at present, lies in allowing self-government to every important group within a nation in all matters that affect that group much more than they affect the rest of the community. The government of a group, chosen by the group, will be far more in touch with its constituents, far more conscious of their interests, than a remote Parliament nominally representing the whole country. The most original idea in Syndicalism—adopted and developed by the Guild Socialists— is the idea of making industries self-governing units so far as their internal affairs are concerned. By this method, extended also to such other groups as have clearly separable interests, the evils which have shown themselves in representative democracy can, I believe, be largely overcome. . . .

There is no method, if we are not mistaken, by which a body representing the whole community, whether as producers or consumers or both, can alone be a sufficient guardian of individual liberty. The only way of preserving sufficient liberty (and even this will be inadequate in the case of very small minorities) is the organization of citizens with special interests into groups, determined to preserve autonomy as regards their internal affairs, willing to resist interference by a strike if necessary, and sufficiently powerful (either in themselves or through their power of appealing to public sympathy) to be able to resist the organized forces of government successfully when their cause is such as many men think just. If this method is to be successful we must have not only suitable organizations but also a diffused respect for liberty, and an absence of submissiveness to government both in theory and practice. Some risk of disorder there must be in such a society, but this risk is as nothing compared to the danger of stagnation which is inseparable from an all-powerful central authority.

We may now sum up our discussion of the powers of Government.

The State, in spite of what Anarchists urge, seems a necessary institution for certain purposes. Peace and war, tariffs, regulation of sanitary conditions and of the sale of noxious drugs, the preservation of a just system of distribution: these, among others, are functions which could hardly be performed in a community in which there was no central government. Take, for example, the liquor traffic, or the opium traffic in China. If alcohol could be obtained at cost price without taxation, still more if it could be obtained for nothing, as Anarchists presumably desire, can we believe that there would not be a great and disastrous increase of drunkenness? China was brought to the verge of ruin by opium, and every patriotic Chinaman desired to see the traffic in opium restricted. In such matters freedom is not a panacea, and some degree of legal restriction seems imperative for the national health.

But granting that the State, in some form, must continue, we must also grant, I think, that its powers ought to be very strictly limited to what is absolutely necessary. There is no way of limiting its powers except by means of groups which are jealous of their privileges and determined to preserve their autonomy, even if this should involve resistance to laws decreed by the State, when these laws interfere in the internal affairs of a group in ways not warranted by the public interest. The glorification of the State, and the doctrine that it is every citizen's duty to serve the State, are radically against progress and against liberty. The State, though at present a source of much evil, is also a means to certain good things, and will be needed so long as violent and destructive impulses remain common. But it is *merely* a means, and a means which needs to be very carefully and sparingly used if it is not to do more harm than good. It is not the State, but the community, the world-wide community of all human beings present and future, that we ought to serve. And a good community does not spring from the glory of the State, but from the unfettered development of individuals: from happiness in daily life, from congenial work giving opportunity for whatever constructiveness each man or woman may possess, from free personal relations embodying love and taking away the roots of envy in thwarted capacity from affection, and above all from the joy of life and its expression in the spontaneous creations of art and science. It is these things that make an age or a nation worthy of existence, and these things are not to be secured by bowing down before the State. It is the individual in whom all that is good must be realized, and the free growth of the individual must be the supreme end of a political system which is to re-fashion the world.

11 An Estimate of Anarchism's Role

JAMES JOLL

James Joll (1918—) is professor of international history at the London School of Economics and Political Science. He is well known for his writings on modern European history, including the history of revolutionary movements. The following is the conclusion to his fine history of anarchism, The Anarchists. *Those wanting to learn more about the subject would do well to read Joll's book, or George Woodcock's* Anarchism *(1962), an excellent history which is rather more comprehensive than Joll's, though perhaps not quite as readable. No other history of anarchism can be recommended.*

"Give flowers to the rebels failed." So runs the first line of an Italian anarchist poem which Vanzetti sat translating in his prison cell. And, as one looks at the repeated failures of anarchism in action, culminating in the tragedy of the Spanish Civil War, one is tempted to strike the same elegiac note. The contradictions and inconsistencies of anarchist theory, the difficulty, if not the impossibility, of putting it into practice all seem illustrated by the experiences of the past hundred and fifty years. Nevertheless, anarchism is a doctrine that has attracted a number of people in each generation, and its ideas still have an appeal, though perhaps more as a personal ethical creed than as a social revolutionary force. Most of

From *The Anarchists* (London: Eyre & Spottiswoode, 1964, and Boston: Atlantic-Little, Brown and Co., 1965), pp. 275–280. Copyright © 1964 by James Joll.

the people who have become anarchists were not self-torturing neurotics—though some of the terrorists undoubtedly were—but people who regarded anarchism as a practical revolutionary ideal and a realizable hope. The philosophical anarchists—a Godwin and even a Proudhon or a Kropotkin—may have come to think that their criticism of existing society was more theoretical than practical and that the system of social values they sought to inculcate was not immediately realizable; but they certainly believed that it might be realized one day. The mass of poor people who, from the 1880s on, accepted anarchism as a basis for action, did so, however, because the total revolution which the anarchists promised seemed to offer an immediate hope of success, and indeed seemed to be the only possibility of improving their desperate condition.

Anarchism is necessarily a creed of all or nothing, and consequently it has had less success in countries where there is still a hope of winning something out of the existing system. When a trade union can successfully negotiate higher wages or better conditions of work, and when political parties are able to introduce measures of reform and to remedy grievances, then the extreme solution of a total revolution seems less desirable. To this extent, Bakunin's belief that the true revolutionaries are those with nothing to lose has been justified. However, anarchism in action has always come up against the fact that, for better or for worse, all the nations of the west—even Russia and Spain, where anarchism seemed to have the best prospects of success—have decided on political action and a centralized government as the means of obtaining the society they want. "The government of man" is no nearer being replaced by "the administration of things" than it was when the utopian socialists put forward the idea in the first half of the last century. The political party, so abhorred by all good anarchists, has become the characteristic organ of twentieth-century government, so that even the dictatorships of the twentieth century have used the single party as a means of exercising their tyranny instead of practicing the undisguised autocracy of earlier periods. Thus, in practice, the anarchists have deliberately dissociated themselves from what the majority of people in the twentieth century have regarded as essential for political and social progress. While their criticism of traditional ideas of state sovereignty, representative government and political reform may have often been valid, and the warnings they have repeatedly issued about the dangers of sacrificing liberty in the supposed interests of the revolution have often been justified, the anarchists have failed to suggest just how their alternative system can be made to work. They have never, that is to say, envisaged any intermediate stage between existing society and the total revolution of their dreams.

In another respect, too, the anarchists have shown themselves opposed to the dominating trends of contemporary economic organization. Mass production and consumption, and large-scale industry under a centralized direction, whether capitalist or socialist, have, whatever one may think about them, become the characteristic forms of western society and of the newly emergent industrial countries elsewhere. It is hard to see how these could be adapted to anarchist ideas about production and exchange; and therefore the anarchists who have envisaged the total destruction of existing society as a preliminary to the erection of a new order are doubtless right. However, the ambivalent attitude of the anarchists toward technological progress has left a corresponding ambivalence in their views of the future society. Although, as we have seen, Godwin and Kropotkin welcomed new inventions which would relieve men of unpleasant and squalid tasks—refuse disposal has always been one of the great problems confronting utopian thinkers—nevertheless, the basic assumptions of anarchism are all contrary to the development of large-scale industry and of mass production and consumption. When it comes to the point, the anarchists are all agreed that in the new society man will live in extreme simplicity and frugality and will be quite happy to do without the technical achievements of the industrial age. For this reason, much anarchist thinking seems to be based on a romantic, backward-looking vision of an idealized past society of artisans and peasants, and on a total rejection of the realities of twentieth-century social and economic organization. While some syndicalist ideals and a degree of workers' control of industry may mitigate some of the inhumanity of large factories, a total destruction of the contemporary structure of industry is scarcely imaginable without violent cataclysm. However, in certain emergency situations such as existed in Russia in 1917 and in Catalonia in 1936, when the governmental and economic machinery has been disrupted or destroyed by war, there might still exist a chance of putting anarchist ideas into practice and of starting to rebuild from nothing a new society on anarchist principles. Perhaps the anarchist revolution could only take place after the total disruption of the means of government, communications, production and exchange by, say, a nuclear war; and perhaps, after all, the terrorists were right, and only a bomb on a larger scale than any they ever envisaged could prepare the way for the true social revolution.

However, in countries where industrial development has not yet conditioned the whole social structure as it has in Europe and North America, the ideals of the anarchists might still seem to be within reach. In India, Gandhi himself and subsequent social reformers such as Jayaprakash Narayan and Vinobha Bhave have dreamed of basing Indian society on (in Gandhi's words) "self-sufficient, self-governing village republics." Perhaps even in India the development of a centralized industrial community has gone too far to be stopped, and Jayaprakash Narayan has realized that the changes he proposes also involve the abandonment of India's western-style parliamentary democracy. Indeed, his attack on liberal parliamentary institutions and his demand for "self-governing, self-sufficient, agro-industrial, urbo-rural local communities" is closely reminiscent of Proudhon. And, like Proudhon, Mr. Narayan is perhaps too optimistic when he thinks that the rejection of liberal institutions will lead to a better form of government. He writes that "The evidence from Cairo to Djakarta indicates that Asian peoples are having second thoughts, and are seeking to find better forms than parliamentary democracy to express and embody their democratic aspirations." What is sad is that the evidence hardly suggests that these new forms have anything in common with Mr. Narayan's admirable

Proudhonian ideals. Indeed, if the Indians with a long tradition of village communities and with the example and teaching of Gandhi, the only twentieth-century statesman with the moral sophistication to make a revolution that was ethical as well as social and political, have not succeeded in starting a social revolution on the lines advocated by Mr. Narayan, it is hard to see who else is likely to do so.

However, if the anarchists have failed to make their revolution and seem even further from doing so today than ever, they have all the same provided a continuous criticism of prevailing views and have occasionally made us think again about our political and social presuppositions. They have consistently pointed out the dangers of making the wrong kind of revolution, and their warnings over the last hundred years that Marxism would lead to dictatorship and to the replacement of the old tyrannies by a new one have been proved all too right. Whatever they may have thought they were doing, the anarchists have, in fact, produced a revolutionary ideal which corresponds exactly to Sorel's myth—"not a description of things but an expression of will." It is by their ruthless and extreme assertion of an uncompromising set of beliefs that the anarchists have set an example and issued a challenge. Like all puritans, they have succeeded in making us just a little uneasy about the kind of life we lead.

Clemenceau once said: "I am sorry for anyone who has not been an anarchist at twenty"; and it is obvious that the ardent and irrepressible optimism of anarchist doctrines will always have an appeal to the young in revolt against the social and moral conceptions of their elders. Yet it is not so much the enthusiasm of youth that has made the anarchist leaders impressive, but rather, in the case of men like Kropotkin or Malatesta, the consistency and devotion with which, in spite of disappointments and in face, it may be thought, of overwhelming contrary evidence, they have maintained into old age their beliefs unchanged and their hopes undimmed. The strength of anarchism has lain in the characters of those who have practiced it; and it is as an austere personal moral and social code that it will continue to attract people who want a total alternative to the values of contemporary society and politics and whose temperaments respond to the appeal of ideas carried to their logical conclusions, regardless of the practical difficulties involved.

There is also another sense in which anarchism, quite apart from its success or failure as a social revolutionary movement, will always find some converts. Certain types of anarchists provide examples of a *jusqu'au boutisme*, an extreme degree of individualist self-assertion, which rejects all conventions and all restrictions. These anarchists practice in their everyday lives the Nietzschean *Umwertung aller Werte*, the overturning of all accepted values. The bohemians of the 1890s are echoed by the beat generation of the 1950s in their protest against the stuffiness and conformity of the bourgeois society in which they have grown up. And, while this sort of revolt often ends in futility and sometimes in personal disaster, it can also produce a revolutionary art which effectively challenges convention and tradition and is truly anarchist in its disruptive effect. The Dada painters and writers, for example, produced an art which, by attacking the idea of art itself, enabled them, as they thought, to escape from values of any kind. Their successors, the surrealists, again asserted their right to complete freedom. As one of their historians put it: "Surrealism has nothing in common with a religious movement. Yet it is the only thing capable of giving man what all religions had provided for him: total liberty of the human being in a liberated world." This desire to assert total individual freedom from all restraints and conventions has its dangers: it can become both trivial and silly. As a leading surrealist, André Breton, remarked: *"Il n'y a rien avec quoi il soit si dangereux de prendre des libertés comme avec la liberté."* A state of permanent rejection of all rules is the most exacting way of life possible, and individualist anarchism, like social anarchism, demands a devotion and austerity which few who practice it attain. (It is not entirely surprising, for instance, that some of the leading surrealists have preferred to turn to the ready-made discipline of the communists rather than to the self-imposed freedom of their original beliefs.) However, just as the revolutionary anarchist thinkers provided a vision of an alternative social order and a challenge to all our accepted political and economic conventions, so the individualist anarchists and the artists whose work has reflected their beliefs have provided a series of salutary shocks to our moral and aesthetic beliefs. The idea of a "morality without obligations or sanctions" is as attractive as that of a society without government or governed; and, in one form or another, each will have its disciples in every generation.

12 The Black Flag of Anarchism

PAUL GOODMAN

Paul Goodman (1911—) is an amazingly versatile humanist and social critic who has written with brilliance and originality in the areas of politics, education, sociology, psychology, urban planning, fiction, and poetry. His perspective is that of an anarchist, but his thought is too broad and fresh for him to be categorized simply as an anarchist. Goodman is probably the most creative and consistently interesting contemporary writer in the anarchist genre.

The wave of student protest in the advanced countries overrides national boundaries, racial differences, the ideological distinctions of fascism, corporate liberalism and communism. Needless to say, officials of the capitalist countries say that the agitators are Communists, and Communists say they are bourgeois revisionists. In my opinion, there is a totally different political philosophy underlying—it is Anarchism.

The actual "issues" are local and often seem trivial. The troubles are usually spontaneous, though there is sometimes a group bent on picking a fight in the brooding unrest. A play is banned, a teacher is fired, a student publication is censored, university courses are not practical or facilities are inadequate, the administration is too rigid, there are restrictions on

From *The New York Times Magazine*, July 14, 1968, pp. 10, 11, 13, 15, 16, 18, 20, 22. Copyright © 1968 by The New York Times Company. Reprinted by permission.

economic mobility or there is technocratic mandarinism, the poor are treated arrogantly, students are drafted for an unjust war—any of these, anywhere in the world, may set off a major explosion, ending with police and broken heads. The spontaneity, the concreteness of the issues, and the tactics of direct action are themselves characteristic of Anarchism.

Historically, Anarchism has been the revolutionary politics of skilled artisans and farmers who do not need a boss; of workmen in dangerous occupations, e.g., miners and lumbermen, who learn to trust one another, and of aristocrats who can economically afford to be idealistic. It springs up when the system of society is not moral, free or fraternal enough. Students are likely to be Anarchists but, in the immense expansion of schooling everywhere, they are new as a mass and they are confused about their position.

Political Anarchism is rarely mentioned and never spelled out in the press and TV. West and East, journalists speak of "anarchy" to mean chaotic riot and aimless defiance of authority; or they lump together "communists and anarchists" and "bourgeois revisionists, infantile leftists and anarchists." Reporting the troubles in France, they have had to distinguish Communists and Anarchists because the Communist labor unions promptly disowned the Anarchist students, but no proposition of the Anarchists has been mentioned except for Daniel Cohn-Bendit's vaunting statement, "I scoff at all national flags!"

(The possibility of an Anarchist revolution—decentralist, anti-police, anti-party, anti-bureaucratic, organized by voluntary association, and putting a premium on grassroots spontaneity—has always been anathema to Marxist Communists and has been ruthlessly suppressed. Marx expelled the Anarchist unions from the International Workingmen's Association; Lenin and Trotsky slaughtered the Anarchists in the Ukraine and at Kronstadt; Stalin murdered them during the Spanish Civil War; Castro has jailed them in Cuba, and Gomulka in Poland. Nor is Anarchism necessarily socialist, in the sense of espousing common ownership. That would depend. Corporate capitalism, state capitalism, and state communism are all unacceptable, because they trap people, exploit them, and push them around. Pure communism, meaning voluntary labor and free appropriation, is congenial to Anarchists. But Adam Smith's economics, in its pure form, is also Anarchist, and was so called in his time; and there is an Anarchist ring to Jefferson's agrarian notion that a man needs enough control of his subsistence to be free of irresistible pressure. Underlying all Anarchist thought is a hankering for peasant independence, craft guild self-management and the democracy of medieval Free Cities. Naturally it is a question how all can be achieved in modern technical and urban conditions. In my opinion, we could go a lot further than we think if we set our sights on decency and freedom rather than delusory "greatness" and suburban "affluence.")

In this country, where we have no continuing Anarchist tradition, the young hardly know their tendency at all. I have seen the black flag of Anarchy at only a single demonstration, when 165 students burned their draft cards on the Sheep Meadow in New York, in April 1967—naturally, the press noticed only the pretentiously displayed Vietcong flags that had no connection with the draft-card burners. (A black flag was also raised along with a red flag at the national convention of Students for a Democratic Society in East Lansing in June [1968].) Recently at Columbia, it was the red flag that waved from the roof. The American young are unusually ignorant of political history. The generation gap, their alienation from tradition, is so profound that they cannot remember the correct name for what they in fact do.

This ignorance has unfortunate consequences for their movement and lands them in wild contradictions. In the United States, the New Left has agreed to regard itself as Marxist and speaks of "seizing power" and "building socialism," although it is strongly opposed to centralized power and it has no economic theory whatever for a society and technology like ours. It is painful to hear students who bitterly protest being treated like

I.B.M. cards, nevertheless defending Chairman Mao's little red book; and Carl Davidson, editor of New Left Notes, has gone so far as to speak of "bourgeois civil liberties." In the Communist bloc, unlike the Latin countries, the tradition is also wiped out. For instance, in Czechoslovakia, Poland, and Yugoslavia, students who want civil liberties and more economic freedom are called bourgeois, although in fact they are disgusted by the materialism of their own regimes and they aspire to workers' management, rural reconstruction, the withering away of the state, the very Anarchism that Marx promised as pie in the sky.

Worst of all, not recognizing what they are, the students do not find one another as an international movement, though they have a common style, tactics and culture. Yet there are vital goals which, in my opinion, can be achieved only by the immense potential power of youth acting internationally. Certainly, as a first order of business, they ought to be acting in concert to ban the nuclear bombs of France, China, Russia, and the United States; otherwise they will not live out their lives.

The protesting students are Anarchist because they are in a historical situation to which Anarchism is their only possible response. During all their lifetime the Great Powers have been in the deadlock of the Cold War, stockpiling nuclear weapons. Vast military-industrial complexes have developed, technology has been abused, science and the universities have been corrupted. Education has turned into processing, for longer years and at a faster pace. Centralized social engineering is creating the world forecast in Orwell's *1984*. Manipulated for national goals they cannot believe in, the young are alienated. On every continent there is excessive urbanization and the world is heading for ecological disaster.

Under these conditions, the young reject authority, for it is not only immoral but functionally incompetent, which is unforgivable. They think they can do better themselves. They want to abolish national frontiers. They do not believe in Great Power. Since they are willing to let the Systems fall apart, they are not moved by appeals to law and order. They believe in local power, community development, rural reconstruction, decentralist organization, so they can have a say. They prefer a simpler standard of living. Though their protests generate violence, they themselves tend to nonviolence and are internationally pacifist. But they do not trust the due process of administrators and are quick to resort to direct action and civil disobedience. All this adds up to the community Anarchism of Kropotkin, the resistance Anarchism of Malatesta, the agitational Anarchism of Bakunin, the Guild Socialism of William Morris, the personalist politics of Thoreau.

The confused tangle of Anarchist and authoritarian ideas was well illustrated by the actions of Students for a Democratic Society in leading the protest at Columbia [in 1968].

The two original issues, to purge the university of the military and to give local power to the Harlem community, were Anarchist in spirit—though, of course, they could be supported by liberals and Marxists as well. The direct action, of nonviolently occupying the buildings, was classically Anarchist.

The issues were not strictly bona fide, however, for the S.D.S. chapter was carrying out a national plan to embarrass many schools during the spring, using any convenient pretexts, in order to attack the System. In itself, this was not unjustifiable, since the big universities, including Columbia, are certainly an important part of our military operations, which ought to be stopped. But the S.D.S. formulation was not acceptable: "Since we cannot yet take over the whole society, let us begin by taking Columbia." I doubt that most of the students who participated wanted to "take over" anything, and I am sure they would have been as restive if ruled by the S.D.S. leadership as by the president and trustees of Columbia.

When the faculty came to life and the students' justified demands began to be taken seriously—in the normal course of events, as has happened on several other campuses, the students would have gone unpunished or been suspended for 45 minutes—S.D.S. suddenly revealed a deeper purpose, to "politicize" the students and "radicalize" the professors by forcing a "confrontation" with the police: if the police had to be called, people would see the System naked. Therefore the leadership raised the ante and made negotiation impossible. The administration was not big-souled enough to take it whence it came, nor patient enough to sit it out; it called the police and there was a shambles.

To have a shambles is not necessarily unjustifiable, on the hypothesis that total disruption is the only way to change a totally corrupt society. But the concept of "radicalizing" is a rather presumptuous manipulation of people for their own good. It is Anarchist for people to act on principle and learn, the hard way, that the powers that be are brutal and unjust, but it is authoritarian for people to be expended for the cause on somebody's strategy. (In my experience, a professional really becomes radical when he tries to pursue his profession with integrity and courage; this is what he knows and cares about, and he soon finds that many things must be changed. In student disturbances, professors have not been "radicalized" to the jejune program of New Left Notes, but they *have* recalled to mind what it means to be a professor at all.)

Ultimately, when four leaders were suspended and students again occupied a building in their support, the S.D.S. tendency toward authority became frankly dictatorial. A majority of the students voted to leave on their own steam before the police came, since there was no sense in being beaten up and arrested again; but the leadership brushed aside the vote because it did not represent the correct position, and the others—I suppose out of animal loyalty—stayed and were again busted.

Nevertheless, the Columbia action was also a model of Anarchism. and the same S.D.S. leaders deserve much of the credit. In the first place, it seems to have halted the university's displacement of poor people, whereas for years citizenly protests (including mine) had accomplished nothing. When, because of police brutality, there was a successful strike and sessions of the college and some of the graduate schools were terminated for the semester, the students rapidly and efficiently made new arrangements with favorable professors for work to go on. They organized a "free university" and brought a host of distinguished outsiders to the campus. A group, Students for a Restructured University, amicably split from S.D.S to devote itself to the arts of peace and work out livable relations with the administration. For a while, until the police came back, the atmosphere on the campus was pastoral. Faculty and students talked to one another. Like Berkeley after its troubles, Columbia was a much better place.

In Anarchist theory, "revolution" means the moment when the structure of authority is loosed, so that free functioning can occur. The aim is to open areas of freedom and defend them. In complicated modern societies it is probably safest to work at this piecemeal, avoiding chaos which tends to produce dictatorship.

To Marxists, on the other hand, "revolution" means the moment in which a new state apparatus takes power and runs things its own way. From the Anarchist point of view, this is "counterrevolution," since there is a new authority to oppose. But Marxists insist that piecemeal change is mere reformism, and one has to seize power and have a strong administration in order to prevent reaction.

At Columbia the administration and the authoritarians in S.D.S. seem to have engaged in an almost deliberate conspiracy to escalate their conflict and make the Marxist theory true. The administration was deaf to just grievances, it did not have to call the police when it did, and it did not have to suspend the students. It has been pigheaded and vindictive. Worse, it has been petty. For instance, during the strike the sprinklers were ordered to be kept going all day, ruining the grass, in order to prevent the students from holding "free university" sessions on the lawn. When a speaker addressed a rally, a sweeper had been instructed to move a noisy vacuum cleaner to the spot to drown him out. William J. Whiteside, the director of buildings and grounds, explained to a *Times* reporter that "these bullhorn congregations lead to an awful lot of litter, so we have to get out there and clean it up." This from a university founded in 1754.

Consider two key terms of New Left rhetoric, "participatory democracy" and "cadres." I think these concepts are incompatible, yet both are continually used by the same youth.

Participatory democracy was the chief idea in the Port Huron Statement, the founding charter of Students for a Democratic Society. It is a cry for a say in the decisions that shape our lives, as against top-down direction, social engineering, corporate and political centralization, absentee owners, brainwashing by mass media. In its connotations, it encompasses no taxation without representation, grass-roots populism, the town meeting, congregationalism, federalism, Student Power, Black Power, workers' management, soldiers' democracy, guerrilla organization. It is, of course, the essence of Anarchist social order, the voluntary federation of self-managed enterprises.

Participatory democracy is grounded in the following social-psychological hypotheses: People who actually perform a function usually best know how it should be done. By and large, their free decision will be efficient, inventive, graceful, and forceful. Being active and self-confident, they will cooperate with other groups with a minimum of envy, anxiety, irrational violence, or the need to dominate.

And, as Jefferson pointed out, only such an organization of society is self-improving; we learn by doing, and the only way to educate cooperative citizens is to give power to people as they are. Except in unusual circumstances, there is not much need for dictators, deans, police, prearranged curricula, imposed schedules, conscription, coercive laws. Free people easily agree among themselves on plausible working rules; they listen to expert direction when necessary; they wisely choose pro tem leaders. Remove authority, and there will be self-regulation, not chaos.

And radical student activity has in fact followed this line. Opposing the bureaucratic system of welfare, students have devoted themselves to community development, serving not as leaders or experts but as catalysts to bring poor people together, so they can become aware of and solve their own problems. In politics, the radical students usually do not consider it worth the trouble and expense to try to elect distant representatives; it is better to organize local groups to fight for their own interests.

In the students' own protest actions, like the Free Speech Movement in Berkeley, there were no "leaders"—except in the TV coverage—or rather there were dozens of pro tem leaders; yet F.S.M. and other such actions have moved with considerable efficiency. Even in immense rallies, with tens of thousands gathering from a thousand miles, as in New York in April, 1967, or at the Pentagon in October 1967, the unvarying rule has been to exclude no groups on "principle," no matter how incompatible their tendencies; despite dire warnings, each group has done its own thing and the whole has been well enough. When it has been necessary to make immediate arrangements, as in organizing the occupied buildings at Columbia or devising new relations with the professors, spontaneous democracy has worked beautifully. In the civil rights movement in the South, Martin Luther King used to point out, each locality planned and carried out its own campaign and the national leadership just gave what financial or legal help it could.

Turn now to "cadres." In the past few years, this term from the vocabulary of military regimentation has become overwhelmingly prevalent in New Left rhetoric, as it was among the various Communist sects in the thirties. (My hunch is that it was the Trotskyists who gave it political currency. Trotsky had been the commander of the Red Army.) A cadre or squad is the primary administrative or tactical unit by which small groups of human beings are transformed into sociological entities, to execute the unitary will of the organization, whether army, political party, work force, labor union, agitation or propaganda machine. In Marxian terms, it is the unit of alienation from human nature, and young Marx would certainly have disapproved.

"Cadre" connotes the breaking down of ordinary human relations and transcending personal motives, in order to channel energy for the cause. For purposes of agitation, it is the Jesuit idea of indoctrinating and training a small band who then go forth and multiply themselves. The officers, discipline, and tactics of military cadres are determined in headquarters; this is the opposite of guerrilla organization, for guerrillas are self-reliant, devise their own tactics, and are bound by personal or feudal loyalty, so that it is puzzling to hear the admirers of Che Guevara use the word "cadres." As a revolutionary political method, cadre-formation connotes the development of a tightly knit conspiratorial party which will eventually seize the system of institutions and exercise a dictatorship until it transforms the majority of its own doctrine and behavior. Etymologically, "cadre" and "squad" come from (Latin) quadrus, a square, with the sense of fitting people into a framework.

Obviously, these connotations are entirely repugnant to the actual motives and spirit of the young at present, everywhere in the world. In my opinion, the leaders who use this language are suffering from a romantic delusion. The young are not conspiratorial but devastatingly open. For instance, when youth of the draft resistance movement are summoned to a grand jury, it is very difficult for their Civil Liberties lawyers to get them to plead the Fifth Amendment. They will sacrifice themselves and get their heads broken, but it has to be according to their personal judgment. They insist on wearing their own garb even if it is bad for Public Relations. Their ethics are even embarrassingly Kantian, so that ordinary prudence and reasonable casuistry are called finking.

And I do not think they want "power" but just to be taken into account, to be able to do their thing, and to be let alone. They indeed want a revolutionary change, but not by this route. Except for a while, on particular occasions, they simply cannot be manipulated to be the shock troops of a Leninist coup. (I have never found that I could teach them anything else either.) If the young go along with actions organized by the Trotskyists or the Progressive Labor Party or some of the delusions of S.D.S., it is because, in their judgment, the resulting disruption does more good than harm. Compared with the arrogance, cold violence and inhumanity of our established institutions, the arrogance, hot-headedness and all-too-human folly of the young are venial.

The trouble with the neo-Leninist wing of the New Left is a different one. It is that the abortive manipulation of lively energy and moral fervor for a political revolution that will not be, and ought not to be, confuses the piecemeal social revolution that is brightly possible. This puts me off—but of course they have to do it their own way. It is inauthentic to do community development in order to "politicize" people, or to use a good do-it-yourself project as a means of "bringing people into the Movement." Everything should be done for its own sake. The amazing courage of sticking to one's convictions in the face of the police is insulted when it is manipulated as a means of "radicalizing." The loyalty and trust in one another of youth is extraordinary, but it can turn to disillusionment if they perceive that they are being had. Many of the best of the young went through this in the thirties. But at least there is no Moscow gold around, though there seems to be plenty of C.I.A. money both at home and abroad.

Finally, in this account of confused Anarchism, we must mention the conflict between the activists and the hippies.

The activists complain that the dropouts are not political and will not change anything. Instead, they are seducers who drastically interfere with the formation of cadres. (We are back to "Religion is the opium of the people" or perhaps "LSD is the opium of the people.") Of course, there is something in this, but in my opinion the bitterness of the New Left polemic against the hippies can only be explained by saying that the activists are defensive against their own repressed impulses.

In fact, the dropouts are not unpolitical. When there is an important demonstration, they are out in force and get beaten up with the rest—though they are not "radicalized." With their flowers and their slogan "Make Love Not War," they provide all of the color and much of the deep meaning. One hippie group, the Diggers, has a full-blown economics, has set up free stores, and has tried to farm, in order to be independent of the System, while it engages in community development.

The Yippies, the Youth International Party (would that it were!), devote themselves to undermining the System; they are the ones who showered dollar bills on the floor of the Stock

Exchange, tied up Grand Central Station, and tried to exorcise the Pentagon with incantations. And the Dutch Provos, the "provotariat," who are less drug-befuddled than the Yippies, improvise ingenious improvements to make society better as a means of tearing it down; they even won an election in Amsterdam.

On their side, the hippies claim that the New Left has gotten neatly caught in the bag of the System. To make a frontal attack is to play according to the enemy's rules, where one doesn't have a chance; and victory would be a drag anyway. The thing is to use jujitsu, ridicule, Schweikism, nonviolent resistance, by-passing, infuriating, tripping up, seducing by offering happy alternatives. A complex society is hopelessly vulnerable, and the fourteen-year-olds run away and join the gypsies.

This criticism of the New Left is sound. A new politics demands a new style, a new personality and a new way of life. To form cadres and try to take power is the same old runaround. The Anarchism of the dropouts is often quite self-conscious. It is remarkable, for instance, to hear Emmet Grogan, the spokesman of the Diggers, make up the theories of Prince Kropotkin right out of his own experiences in Haight-Ashbury, the Lower East Side, and riot-torn Newark.

But I think the dropouts are unrealistic in their own terms. Living among the poor, they up the rents. Trying to live freely, they offend the people they want to help. Sometimes blacks and Spanish-Americans have turned on them savagely. In my observation, the "communication" that they get with drugs is illusory, and to rely on chemicals in our technological age is certainly to be in a bag. Because the standard of living is corrupt, they opt for voluntary poverty, but there are also many useful goods that they have a right to, and needlessly forgo. And they are often plain silly.

The more sophisticated Provos have fallen for a disastrous vision of the future, New Babylon, a society in which all will sing and make love and do their thing, while the world's work is done by automatic machines. They do not realize that in such a society power will be wielded by the technocrats, and they themselves will be colonized like Indians on a reservation.

In general, I doubt that it is possible to be free, to have a say, and to live a coherent life, without doing worthwhile work, pursuing the arts and sciences, practicing the professions, bringing up children, engaging in politics. Play and personal relations are a necessary background; they are not what men live *for*. But maybe I am old fashioned, Calvinistic.

For Further Reading

The following are among the most interesting books of major anarchist writers.

Bakunin, Mikhail. *The Political Philosophy of Bakunin*, edit. G. P. Maximoff (New York: The Free Press, 1953). A compilation of extracts to constitute a systematic exposition of his ideas; Bakunin himself wrote only short pieces.

Goodman, Paul. *People or Personnel* and *Like a Conquered Province* (New York: Vintage, 1968). A paperback edition of two books, with seven additional essays.

Kropotkin, Peter. *Kropotkin's Revolutionary Essays*, edit. Roger Baldwin (New York: Vanguard Press, 1927). His pamphlets, most of them collected here, include much of the theory he develops at greater length in other books.

Malatesta, Errico. *Life and Ideas*, edit. Vernon Richards (London: Freedom Press, 1965). Like the Bakunin volume, a compilation of the ideas of a major anarchist revolutionary who did not stop to write long books.

Proudhon, Pierre-Joseph. *General Idea of the Revolution in the Nineteenth Century* (London: Freedom Press, 1923; Ann Arbor, Mich.: University Microfilms, 1967 [Xerox reproduction]). His best book in English. His *De la Justice dans la Révolution et dans l'Eglise* (Paris: Rivière, 1930), 4 vols., is the most important of all anarchist works.

Read, Herbert. *Anarchy and Order* (London: Faber, 1954). Read was the leading English exponent of a moderate anarchist philosophy.

Index